BEAUMONT'S UP AND UNDER

Trivial Delights from the World of Rugby Union

Printed and bound in Great Britain by MPG Books Ltd, Bodmin

Distributed in the US by Publishers Group West

Arcane is an imprint of Sanctuary Publishing Limited
Sanctuary House, 45–53 Sinclair Road
London W14 0NS, United Kingdom

www.sanctuarypublishing.com

Cover: Ash
Illustrations: BrindeauMexter

ISBN: 1-86074-624-1

BEAUMONT'S UP AND UNDER

Trivial Delights from the World of Rugby Union

Bill Beaumont OBE with Mark Baldwin

arcane

— FOREWORD —

The game of rugby football is, in my opinion, the greatest team game in sport, and has produced more characters than most sports. I suppose I feel this way because, back when the game was played at amateur level, when you got into the dressing room it was full of individuals with different jobs, backgrounds and lives, but their social differences were irrelevant and all were equal. In the current days of professional players, video analysts and squads of trainers and coaches, things are a little different, but nonetheless there are still moments of humour and passion to be found both away from and in front of the cameras.

Thanks to Mark Baldwin's painstaking research, collated here are many interesting and funny stories springing from the world of rugby union, along with a lot of fascinating trivia about the evolution of the game and the stalwart individuals who play it. Having got a majority of my rugby questions wrong on the BBC's *A Question Of Sport* programme, this book would have been perfect for my research, and having worked, listened to and admired many of the characters included in these pages, I can only nod my head and grin in agreement at some of the anecdotes and interviews recorded here. For instance, I've worked with Bill McLaren, and it's true that only he could describe a scrum-half as having more tricks than a bag of weasels!

Rugby has changed considerably since becoming a professional sport, with levels of skill and fitness on a continual upward slide. We have European Club competitions and, of course, the Rugby World Cup, a development that has revitalised the game and opened it up to a whole new audience. And with this new audience comes a hunger for facts, history and stories. To this end, I can only thank Mark Baldwin for writing such a fine and useful book.

Bill Beaumont
January 2005

— INTRODUCTION AND ACKNOWLEDGEMENTS —

Rugby union's journey from ancient ball-gaming, medieval inter-village football and public-school-driven sporting rivalry, to the past century's remarkable growth from amateur pastime to professional big business, has been a riveting and often rollicking ride. I hope that this dip into the wonderful world of rugby, and its fascinating and vivid history, is as entertaining and as varied in its appeal as the game itself.

Rugby is a sport to be enjoyed on various levels, both from a playing point of view and from the perspective of those who simply love to watch it or enthuse about it over a pint or three. But what would the Roman legionnaires who played *harpastum* with such relish, or the Welsh *cnapan* revellers, or the participants in the original local Derby, or even dear old William Webb Ellis himself, have made of the modern international sport of rugby union, with its speed and bravery and cut-and-thrust? The Romans, I fancy, would have especially enjoyed the need for teamwork, organisation and fitness as much as the requirement for individual brilliance and skill. However, rugby is a game that still has much to offer in the 'old-fashioned' amateur arenas of school and club, and this book is as much a celebration of those who nurture the grass roots of the game as those who breathe its rarefied air.

I'd like to pass on my thanks to Bill Beaumont – one of the giants of the game – for his contributions to this project. There is, quite deliberately, a sizeable Lions flavour stirred into the pot-pourri of the following pages, and all good wishes go to Bill and the 2005 British Isles party for their tour to New Zealand.

I would also like to thank Chris Harvey at Sanctuary for his sound advice and invaluable input in terms of the production of the book, and to Peter Bills for his contribution. Some reference points have been acknowledged in the text, but the following volumes have been particular sources of inspiration: *Rothman's Rugby Union Yearbook* (various editions), *Playfair Rugby Union Annual* (various editions), *The Times* and *The Sunday Times* newspapers, *Fotheringham's Sporting Trivia* by Will Fotheringham (Sanctuary Publishing), *The History Of The Rugby World Cup* by Gerald Davies (Sanctuary Publishing), *The Complete Guide To Rugby Union* (Carlton Books) and *Rugby's Strangest Matches* (Robson Books).

Long may rugby union continue to excite, entertain, enthuse and evolve!

Mark Baldwin
January 2005

— OUT ON THEIR FEET —

The 1989 tour of the north of England by Corby Rugby Club became such a success, socially, that they were literally incapable of completing one match. Playing Whitby after a particularly memorable late night, the Corby team soon found themselves trailing by 80 points to 0 – and with just seven minutes of the second half gone at that stage. The referee, exercising a curious mixture of punishment and clemency, abandoned the game, ruling that most of the Corby players were still too drunk. Players and officials then retired to the bar.

— HYPHEN HELL —

Beaten by England's Phil Horrocks-Taylor in the move that nailed Ireland's 1958 defeat at Twickenham, fly-half Mick English was at a loss to explain just how he had failed to tackle his opposite number. 'Well, Horrocks went one way, Taylor went the other and I was left holding the hyphen,' said English.

— IN MEMORIAM 1 —

The Northampton three-quarter Edgar Mobbs was killed at Passchendaele during the First World War when he led his men over the top by kicking a rugby ball into no man's land and chasing after it. Nine days after the start of the War in August 1914, the Rugby Football Union had sent out a circular to all its member clubs which urged all rugby players to enlist.

Rugby was the sport that suffered the greatest casualty rate, pro rata, in the ensuing conflict. Historian Richard Holt wrote, 'They came tumbling out of the public-school clubs, straight off to the trenches to be shot down.' On the last day of the season in 1914, for instance, just months before the outbreak of war, London Scottish fielded four teams comprising 60 men. By 1918, 45 of that number were dead.

— TWICKERS —

The RFU bought Twickenham for the princely sum of £5,573 in 1907. The first club game to be played at the new ground was Harlequins v Richmond in 1909, and the first international staged there was England v Wales in January 1910.

— THE TRY THAT MOVED NATIONS —

The International Rugby Board came into fruition in 1887 largely as a result of a long-running dispute between Scotland and England over the legality of a match-winning try.

The incident had occurred at Blackheath in 1884, the year in which all four home nations played against each other for the first time. The International Championship of that season was, therefore, widely seen as the most important there had ever been, and the title itself was to be decided by the clash between England and Scotland – both unbeaten at that point – in March.

A crowd of more than 8,000 saw the Scots take the lead through an unconverted try, and at half-time they still led. Early in the second half, though, came the moment that led to such weighty ramifications. Scotland were awarded a scrummage near their own line, but a forward by the name of Charles Berry fumbled the ball and knocked it backwards. An English player, Charles Gurdon, seized the loose ball, surged towards the Scottish line and then made a try-scoring pass to Richard Kindersley, a fellow forward.

Appeals to the referee were allowed at this time, however, and the Scots duly asked for the try to be disallowed. They argued that their own knock-back had been illegal, as it was in Scotland, but the English pointed out to referee George Scriven of Ireland that such knock-backs were perfectly legal in England. They added that it was unfair if the Scots were seen to benefit from their own error. The advantage law, however, did not come into the game for another dozen years, and a ten-minute break in the match ensued while the issue was debated.

In the end, referee Scriven ruled in England's favour and Wilfrid Bolton stepped up to kick the goal that clinched both the match and the championship. Scotland were incensed, and afterwards refused to accept the result, saying that the RFU should not have the sole rights to the interpretation of the laws. The 1885 fixture between Scotland and England was cancelled, and in 1886 the Irish Rugby Union (founded in 1879) proposed that an International Board be formed so that consistent laws could be agreed and framed, and so that all disputes could be set before it, as an independent body. At a meeting in Dublin, in 1886, Scotland subsequently agreed to acknowledge the result of the 1884 Blackheath match – two years after the event.

— HOW GARETH GOT THE BLAME —

Certain Welshmen on the 1977 Lions tour to New Zealand later revealed that they felt one man was to blame for the loss of the Test series: the great Gareth Edwards, who at the last minute decided not to make the tour. Had Edwards been there, most felt, the Lions would have strolled to victory, given their huge forward supremacy, and this was probably true, but blaming someone thousands of miles away on the other side of the world seemed a bit harsh at the time, and still does.

— OH, MONSIEUR! —

At Twickenham, in 1985, France wing Patrick Esteve cost his team victory in their Five Nations Championship match against England. Esteve crossed the try line near the corner flag, but then tried to get as close to the posts as possible in order to simplify the conversion. But a quick-thinking England player tackled him, knocking the ball from his grasp. The try was lost, and the game ended in a 9–9 draw.

— THERE'S A FIRST TIME FOR EVERYTHING —

Newton Abbot, England and British Lions forward Denys Dobson was killed by a charging rhinoceros in 1916. He was working as a farmer in Nyasaland at the time. During his rugby career, he had claimed another first when he was sent off in a major match for using 'obscene language' towards the referee.

— TURNING A BLIND EYE —

The 1993 Coal Board Cup tie between Daw Mill from Warwickshire and the Nottinghamshire team of Silverhill Colliery was held up when one of the Silverhill forwards lost his glass eye. Steve Bush, who had lost his natural left eye in a pit accident three years earlier, felt his false eye pop out of its socket during a scrummage. Both sets of players scrabbled around on their hands and knees for several minutes, searching for the missing eye in the muddy turf, but it remained hidden from sight. Bush therefore played on with an empty eye socket, but his heroics could not prevent Daw Mill from emerging 17–8 winners.

— HIGHS AND LOWS 1 —

Tallest and shortest players in the Zurich Premiership:

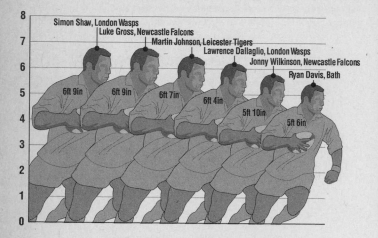

Simon Shaw, London Wasps
Luke Gross, Newcastle Falcons
Martin Johnson, Leicester Tigers
Lawrence Dallaglio, London Wasps
Jonny Wilkinson, Newcastle Falcons
Ryan Davis, Bath

6ft 9in 6ft 9in 6ft 7in 6ft 4in 5ft 10in 5ft 6in

— KING JOHN THE SUPERSTAR —

Barry John, the legendary Wales and British Lions fly-half, won the very first British Superstars event in 1973. John came first in a 100m sprint at the Crystal Palace Athletics Stadium, a race that also involved footballer Bobby Moore, tennis player Roger Taylor, golfer Tony Jacklin, boxer Joe Bugner and racing driver Jackie Stewart.

— THE GREAT ALL-ROUNDER —

Was legendary English sportsman CB Fry the greatest rugby-playing all-rounder of all time? Charles Burgess Fry (1872–1956) played first-class rugby for the Barbarians; he won 26 Test cricket caps for England, as well as captaining them; he played soccer for England; and he equalled the world record for the long jump. He later acted as a delegate to the League of Nations and was invited to become King of Albania. The latter was the one honour he passed up.

— NEW BALL, PLEASE? —

In November 1980, a match between Argentine club side Tucuman and the touring Fijians had to be abandoned when the Fiji fly-half kicked the ball so far out of the ground that it could not be found. A second ball was not in good enough condition, and no one could find another ball.

— WHEN ENGLISH SOIL WAS WELSH —

Everyone remembers when the Wales national team played a number of international matches 'at home' at Wembley Stadium in London in the late 1990s, during the building of the Millennium Stadium in Cardiff. But how many people would know that this was Wales' second 'home' venue on English soil? The first was Birkenhead, in 1887, when Wales offered to entertain Ireland there in order to minimise travelling expenses for the Irish Rugby Union.

— THE BALL —

A 'rugby football' made by William Gilbert was displayed at the 1851 International Exhibition in London. Gilbert balls are still used today.

— THE REF WHO SENT HIMSELF OFF —

A mass brawl that broke out during the Bristol v Newport match of 14 September 1985 led to the referee, George Crawford, walking off the field and leaving the players to it. A qualified local official was found in the crowd, and he took over for the remainder of the game.

— BIRTH OF THE WOODWARD ERA —

Clive Woodward's historic era in charge of England began with a 15–15 draw against Australia in the autumn of 1997. That international featured five new England caps: Will Greenwood, Matt Perry, Andy Long, David Rees and Will Green. In 1998 there were four captains in charge of his England teams: Lawrence Dallaglio, Tony Diprose, Matt Dawson and Martin Johnson.

— THE LONG JOURNEY FROM AMATEURISM —

Rugby Union turned fully and transparently professional only in August 1995, following the third World Cup, when it declared itself officially an open sport. Until that point, the International Rugby Football Board had been dominated for much of its 109-year history by the views and wishes of the 'four home unions': Scotland, Ireland, Wales and England. Indeed, England, who joined the IRFB four years later than the other three home countries, in 1890, enjoyed 6 votes out of 12 until 1911, when their quota was reduced to four votes in order to ensure that there could be no effective veto. Australia, New Zealand and South Africa did not join the IRFB until 1949, when England's voting power was further reduced to two, and from 1949 to 1958 the three 'dominions' had only one vote each.

France joined the IRFB as late as 1978, and by this time all member nations exercised two votes apiece. The four home nations still acted as the senior members, however, and for some time resisted the concept of a World Cup tournament, in the same way that they had resisted the setting up of any sort of competitive domestic league systems in England, Wales, Scotland and Ireland.

The rest of England's break with the Northern Union in 1895, following a row over 'broken time' payments for those needing to miss work in order to play, had not only produced rugby league but also deepened the sense of importance that the amateur game should retain its almost religious beliefs of playing for enjoyment and honour of the jersey and of the game. Even though properly competitive and organised domestic leagues began in the British Isles in the late 1980s, it wasn't until 1993 that the Five Nations Championship became an official event. Up until then, it had officially been a series of 'friendlies', in the minds of home unions administrators, and a feeling lingered among some that agreeing to play in an official tournament was contrary to the ethos of amateur playing, because it brought with it an obligation (rather than an acceptance of an invitation) to play other nations. Increased commercialism, however, and the growing power of television, could have only one result. Ultimately, money talked, even within rugby union's most reactionary bunkers.

— THE FIRST MATCH OF THE FIRST WORLD CUP —

Eden Park in Auckland was only half full for the opening match of the 1987 tournament. The game was between New Zealand and Italy, but it took place on a Friday afternoon – a working day – and there was an obvious imbalance between the two countries that was duly reflected in a final score of 70–6 to the All Blacks.

The choice of this match to lead off the event was, however, symbolic: the game's established power against the bright new future of an expanded sport. This was, don't forget, a largely uncommercial tournament; there were no big sponsors, and only late on did KDD – a Japanese communications company – come on board as a main sponsor. The other supporting sponsors were Rank Xerox, Steinlager and Mazda.

WHAT THEY SAID ABOUT THE FIRST
— RUGBY WORLD CUP —

- IAN McGEECHAN (SCOTLAND COACH): 'We were all excited by it, but not over-serious. No one was quite sure what to make of it all. In Scotland, before we left, there was reluctance about the tournament. It was probably overdue, but there remained a feeling that rugby was being railroaded into something that was not entirely fully supported.'

- JOHN KENDALL-CARPENTER (CHAIRMAN OF THE IRFB TOURNAMENT COMMITTEE): 'This is an historic occasion for rugby union, with 16 nations being brought together for the first time to play in a truly international rugby tournament. It is important for future World Cups, and for rugby itself, that it presents a positive and attractive face to the rest of the sporting world. Equally, it is important that this be a happy occasion which embodies one of the greatest qualities of what we consider to be one of the greatest team games: the camaraderie and the goodwill that is created in the club rooms after the match.'

- SERGE BLANCO (SCORER OF THRILLING LAST-MINUTE WINNING TRY FOR FRANCE IN A MAGNIFICENT SEMI-FINAL AGAINST AUSTRALIA): 'That kind of match, where anything and everything might happen, is the sort of game that I hope tomorrow's rugby will give us. After the match, we were the happiest men in the whole world. By the time we had changed and showered, the stadium was in complete darkness. We went out on to the pitch, did a lap of honour and we sang. We sang Basque songs for half an hour. It was a way of re-experiencing the emotions through our voices, the instrument of feelings. No one else was there. It was our little secret. It was a moment of sheer magic – so happy, so proud of what we had done. It was our special time.'

WHAT THEY SAID ABOUT THE FIRST
— RUGBY WORLD CUP (CONT'D) —

- SEAN FITZPATRICK (WORLD CUP-WINNING NEW ZEALAND HOOKER AND FUTURE CAPTAIN): 'We had a good run throughout. We were miles ahead of all the other countries in terms of fitness and preparation. Our skill levels were greater, too, at that stage. It built a confidence in knowing that no one could get near you. We grew and grew so that, by 1988 and 1989, we were unbeatable, really.'

— WHAT THE F... —

An unfortunate misprint in the France v Ireland international in 1980 meant that the surname of the Irish back-row forward Colm Tucker was spelt with an F instead of a T.

— THAT'S YOUR LOT —

In 1877, the West Wales Challenge Cup final between Cardiff and Llanelli was abandoned because the crowd stole the ball.

— GRANNYGATE —

Eligibility rows have been an almost constant feature of international rugby in recent times, forcing the IRB to tighten up its regulations. All countries have pushed the eligibility question to the limit, seemingly finding players with parents or grandparents who perhaps once set foot in a transit lounge or something. Perhaps the most notorious incident in recent years has been the Wales 'Grannygate' affair of 2000, involving full back Shane Howarth and flanker Brett Sinkinson. Both were suspended after it was discovered that neither Kiwi-born-and-bred player had Welsh ancestry, as had been claimed, and had thus been representing Wales under false pretences.

— A BAD TRIP —

France international player Jean-Pierre Salut was carried off injured before he even made it onto the field for the 1969 match against Scotland in Paris. He tripped as he ran up the stairs that led from the dressing room to the pitch and broke his ankle.

— RACE AGAINST TIME —

Bristol hooker Sam Tucker played 27 times for England between the wars, with by far the most dramatic appearance being when he made a late, mad dash to Cardiff for the 1930 international against Wales.

Tucker had initially been dropped for the game, but his replacement, Douglas Kendrew, was moved to prop when Exeter's Henry Rew was injured in training on the day before the match. The England selectors, however, did not rule Rew out until the morning of the game and sent out an emergency call to Tucker, a First World War veteran who had been injured at the Battle of the Somme. There was no Severn Bridge in those days, of course, and Tucker's fraught journey from Bristol to Cardiff has entered folklore.

When Tucker received the news, he found he had missed the last train that could have carried him from Bristol to Cardiff in time. In desperation, he fixed up a flight from Filton Airport in a private plane. The light aircraft, however, had to land in a field near Cardiff, as there was no landing strip nearby. Tucker, who had never flown before, was badly shaken up by the bumpy landing, but by now he was so determined to make the match that he ran across two fields to the nearest road, where he flagged down a passing lorry. The kindly driver took him to within hailing distance of the ground, but the milling thousands of spectators gathering for the game made getting to the stadium itself a difficult job. By chance, Tucker spotted a policeman he knew and got himself escorted through the throng to the main gates. Sprinting to the England dressing room, he joined his team-mates just five minutes before the scheduled kick-off.

Tucker's epic journey was not without reward, and he contributed fully to an 11–3 victory. Indeed, Tucker had only one regret in the aftermath of this extraordinary episode: Bath's Norman Matthews – the original travelling reserve who had been passed over in favour of Tucker's late call to arms, but who had then been changed and ready to play when it was feared the Bristolian would not make it in time – never received an England cap.

— GOING ON STRIKE —

Play in the international between the United States Eagles and France at Colorado Springs on 20 July 1991 was abandoned just after half-time, with the French 10–3 ahead. The reason for this downing of tools? The ground's main scoreboard was struck by lightning.

— WADE TO GO —

Gregory Wade should never have played for England against Wales in 1882, let alone score three tries in the international. But Wade got his chance as a late call-up because Blackheath forward Philip Newton got lost on his way to the ground in Swansea and missed the game.

— SAFE HANDS —

Cornish second-row line-out specialist Andy Reed, who played club rugby for Bath and Wasps in the 1980s and '90s, and international rugby for Scotland, once played soccer for Bodmin Town in the South Western League as a goalkeeper.

— FAST START —

It took John Leslie, of Scotland, just 10.8 seconds to open the scoring with a try in the 1999 Five Nations Championship international against Wales.

— BACK SOON —

It could only have happened to Ireland. During their 1975 tour to New Zealand, the Irish national team stopped off at Fiji to play a game against the islanders…only to find that the Fijians were on tour in Australia.

— THE JEFFREY–RICHARDS AFFAIR —

One of rugby's most celebrated stories of high jinks occurred following England's 9–6 Five Nations Championship victory against Scotland at Murrayfield in 1988. Opposing back row players Dean Richards, of England, and John Jeffrey, of Scotland, decided to go out for a trawl of Edinburgh's lively pubs on the Saturday night after the match – taking with them the Calcutta Cup. Towards the end of the evening, the Cup was used as a football during a drink-induced kickabout along Prince's Street. The result was damage costing £1,000 to repair, while one wag declared that it now looked more like the Calcutta Plate. Richards received a one-match ban from the RFU, but the Scottish Rugby Union suspended Jeffrey for six months and were dismayed that their English counterparts had not meted out a similarly swingeing punishment.

— IT'S ALL WELSH —

Legendary Wales half-back partners Gareth Edwards and Barry John always spoke to each other in Welsh during international matches in order to keep their tactics private.

— 'A FINE DISREGARD FOR THE RULES' —

The very first rugby player, William Webb Ellis, is defined as something of a rebel by the plaque at Rugby School, which marks the moment when their most famous pupil was supposed to have started a whole new ball game. The plaque reads:

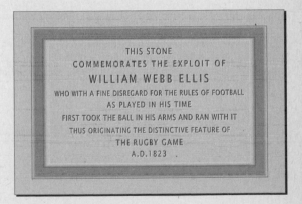

THIS STONE
COMMEMORATES THE EXPLOIT OF
WILLIAM WEBB ELLIS
WHO WITH A FINE DISREGARD FOR THE RULES OF FOOTBALL
AS PLAYED IN HIS TIME
FIRST TOOK THE BALL IN HIS ARMS AND RAN WITH IT
THUS ORIGINATING THE DISTINCTIVE FEATURE OF
THE RUGBY GAME
A.D. 1823

— PIG'S BLADDER —

In reality, rugby football owes its existence more to the legacy of the medieval inter-village contests, in which a rudimentary ball made from an inflated pig's bladder was kicked, thrown and carried over rough terrain in an attempt to score 'goals'. These highly violent mass matches, often contested by hundreds of people on either side, were the forerunners of both rugby and football.

— WILLIE JOHN McBRIDE —

One man above all others deserves the accolade of 'Mr British Lions'. Willie John McBride, of Ballymena and Ireland, made his first Lions tour in 1962, to South Africa, following this four years later with a trip to New Zealand with the 1966 Lions. In 1968, he returned to South Africa with another Lions party, and followed that tour three years later with a further tour of New Zealand with John Dawes' great 1971 Lions side. In 1974, he was chosen to captain the Lions on what proved to be a record-breaking tour of the Republic.

But McBride's association with the Lions didn't end there, even after five tours as a player. In 1983, he was asked to manage that year's Lions on their tour of New Zealand, giving him an astonishing sixth trip.

In all, McBride won a record-breaking 17 Test caps with the Lions between 1962 and 1974. The closest anyone has come to that tally is Dickie Jeeps, England scrum-half of the 1950s and 1960s, who won 13 caps on Lions tours in 1955, 1959 and 1962. In more recent times, Graham Price won 12 caps as a prop-forward on Lions tours in 1977, 1980 and 1983, and indeed played in every Test match on those three tours.

The 1974 British Lions, captained by McBride, established many notable records. The tour became the most successful Lions tour ever, amassing a whopping 729 points on their unbeaten march into the record books. They also scored 107 tries, including 16 in a single game: the 97–0 thrashing of South West Districts at Mossel Bay. Flying wing JJ Williams of Wales bagged six tries that day, while another Williams – full back JPR – nabbed two. England fly-half Alan Old converted 15 of the 16 touchdowns.

Sadly, just two games later, Old was badly late-tackled in the Lions' match against the Proteas at Cape Town and suffered a severed knee ligament. He was flown home a few weeks later and never played for the Lions again.

— SYD MILLAR —

While Willie John McBride has played the most Tests ever for the Lions and enjoyed a spell of unmatched longevity in his association with them, his fellow Irishman and Ballymena club player Syd Millar was almost as successful.

Millar's involvement with the Lions began in 1959, when he was chosen for the tour of Australia and New Zealand. In 1962, he accompanied Arthur

Smith's Lions to South Africa and, in 1968, went back to South Africa with a Lions squad captained by fellow Irishman Tom Kiernan.

That was the end of Millar's playing association with the Lions but by no means the conclusion of his involvement. In 1974, as coach, he helped to mastermind the triumph of McBride's unbeaten Lions in South Africa, and then, six years later, he was appointed manager of the 1980 British Lions – skippered by Bill Beaumont – in South Africa. That tour became Millar's fourth Lions trip to South Africa alone, an extraordinary achievement.

In all, while McBride had been associated with the Lions from 1962 to 1983, Millar's own association stretched (intermittently) from 1962 to 1980. No other men have enjoyed such a long time-span of tours with the British Lions, over so many years.

— OLDEST FIXTURE —

The oldest annual fixture in the game, between Edinburgh Academicals and Merchiston School, was played for the first time in 1858.

— TOUGH CALL —

Kieran Roche, playing for Saracens at Bath in the Zurich Premiership, came on as a replacement forward in the 76th minute and was sent off less than two minutes later by referee Ashley Rowden for 'persistent infringement'.

— SHORT FORM —

The word *scrum*, or *scrummage*, is a shortened form of the word *skirmish*.

— MAGNIFICENT SEVEN —

The triumphant 1971 British Isles tour of New Zealand, on which the Lions lost only one of the 24 matches they played there – the second Test in Christchurch – contained no fewer than seven players from London Welsh. This septet was SJ Dawes (captain), JPR Williams, TGR Davies, TM Davies, J Taylor, MG Roberts and TG Evans. In all, the squad featured 14 Welshmen.

— WORLD CUP VENUES: EUROPE —

— FLY-HALF FACTORY —

Barry John is one of the remarkable quartet of world-class fly-halves produced by Gwendraeth Grammar School in West Wales. John attended the school after Carwyn James, and before both Jonathan Davies and Gareth Davies.

— HEADLINE NEWS —

Rugby is ranked fourth (behind horse-riding, judo and boxing) in the list of sports most likely to cause head injuries to its participants.

— TOP 20 MOST CAPPED INTERNATIONAL PLAYERS* —

1	Jason Leonard (England)	114
2	Philippe Sella (France)	111
3	George Gregan (Australia)	106
4	David Campese (Australia)	101
5	Fabien Pelous (France)	96
6	Serge Blanco (France)	93
7	Sean Fitzpatrick (New Zealand)	92
	Gareth Llewellyn (Wales)	92
9	Joost van der Westhuizen (South Africa)	89
10	Neil Jenkins (Wales)	87
11	Rolando Martin (Argentina)	86
	Joe Roff (Australia)	86
	John Eales (Australia)	86
14	Alessandro Troncon (Italy)	85
	Rory Underwood (England)	85
16	Carlo Checchinato (Italy)	84
	Martin Johnson (England)	84
	Lisandro Arbizu (Argentina)	84
19	Gregor Townsend (Scotland)	82
20	Matthew Burke (Australia)	81

As at 1 January 2005

— WHEELER'S RECORD —

Leicester hooker Peter Wheeler captained two different sides – the Midland Counties and England – to victory over the All Blacks inside ten days in 1983.

— THE LEGACY OF 1871 —

The Rugby Football Union (RFU) was formed in 1871, with an Old Rugbeian (Algernon Rutter) elected as its first president. Also in this year, at Raeburn Place in Edinburgh, the first international between England and Scotland took place, the Scots winning the 20-a-side match by a goal and a try to one try.

— RUGBY PREHISTORY —

The first record of 'a famous game of ball' being played in London was made in 1175, but the origins of rugby go back even further before the day in 1823 when William Webb Ellis picked up the ball and ran with it in a football game being played at Rugby School. Ball games, of some sort or another, are almost as old as human history itself, and there are accounts of two-sided battles played out with ball-type objects going back to ancient civilisations in China, Japan and Greece.

The Romans no doubt drew on these games when they came up with a popular ball game known as *harpastum*. It is known that Roman legions stationed in Britain played this game, and it was clearly used both as a way of keeping the soldiers amused and of helping to keep them fit and hardened to the bumps and bruises of physical combat. It was played with a small, round leather ball – stuffed full of cloth or feathers – that was passed from hand to hand between players. The games were played on a large rectangular 'field', and the objective of two opposing teams was to carry the ball over each other's goal line by force or guile. Tackling was an important aspect of harpastum, and players took up fixed positions on the field. A number of tactical ploys were used, such as dummying to pass.

Probable successors to harpastum evolved over the centuries in various parts of the British Isles. The medieval chronicler Fitzstephen revealed that 'foote balle' of one form or another was tremendously popular in many areas of Britain in the 1100s. He described games of village versus village that seemed more akin to free-for-alls or unarmed combat that could last for days at a time and involve many hundreds of participants over fields of play that often were literally many square miles in size. Indeed, football games were played throughout Europe by the time the Middle Ages came to a close, and many variations survived until quite modern times. For instance, some Irish historians claim that, on that famous day at Rugby, William Webb Ellis was merely demonstrating a game called *caid*, an Irish version of free-for-all football that he must surely have witnessed as a boy when his soldier father was posted to Ireland.

In Cornwall there was a game called *hurling to goales*, in the West Country there was *hurling over country*, in East Anglia *camp ball* and in Wales *cnapan*. The French played *la soule*, or *chole*, and in Florence, Italy, there was a game called *calcio* which attracted large crowds and sounds uncannily rugby-like. What's more, calcio is still played in Florence, in a deliberate upholding of tradition. Even four centuries ago, or more, games of calcio lasted for 50 minutes and were played by two sides of 27 players, made up of 15 forwards and 12 backs. The ball was carried, passed and fought over, and games were staged on piazza 'pitches' very similar in dimensions to modern rugby fields. There is even a painting dating from the 1600s that shows a game of calcio, in which the forwards are clearly disputing possession of the ball, and the backs are lined up behind them waiting for the ball to be passed out.

Meanwhile, street football lasted in Neath, in West Wales, until 1884, and the last organised game of cnapan was played in 1922 between the villages of Llandysul and Llanwenog.

— THE CLUB —

Blackheath, formed in 1858, have always referred to themselves as 'The Club' – in other words, England's original rugby club.

— THE AFTERSHAVE INCIDENT —

England's Cornish prop Colin Smart will forever be remembered in rugby circles as the man who drank a bottle of aftershave at an after-match dinner. The incident took place in Paris, following an international, and was sparked off by the English players each being presented with a bottle of aftershave as a gift from their hosts. Some surreptitiously emptied their bottles and filled them up again with water. Smart, unaware of what they had done, was then challenged to down his bottle quicker than the others.

Sadly, the practical joke almost had tragic consequences. Smart rapidly became ill and had to be rushed off to hospital to have his stomach pumped. Still, it has caused much mirth since and has certainly given Smart more than his 15 minutes of fame. After a fine win over Wales a month later, England scrum-half Steve Smith quipped, 'The aftershave will sure taste good tonight!'

— SHIRT TRIBUTE —

West Hartlepool 'retired' their number-five shirt forever in 1992 as a mark of respect and as a memorial to their lock forward John Howe, who collapsed and died during a league match.

— WHEN THE BOOT TURNED TO BOOS —

In Dunedin in 1959, the Lions Test side captained by Irishman Ronnie Dawson was cruelly robbed by the boot of New Zealand full back Don Clarke. That day the Lions scored four tries to none, yet a remarkable six penalty goals by Clarke squeezed New Zealand home to an 18–17 victory.

Even the New Zealand critics were ashamed to applaud a victory in such circumstances, the late TP McLean dismissing the win as 'a day best forgotten in the annals of All Black history'.

— BILL McLAREN'S FAVOURITE SAYINGS —

1   About a large stampeding forward: 'There goes 18 stones of prime Scottish/Welsh/Irish/English beef on the hoof.'

2   About a nippy, zig-zagging back (usually Simon Geoghegan): 'He's like a mad ferret.'

3   About a nippy, crafty, sniping scrum-half: 'He's got more tricks than a bag of weasels.'

4   About the likely reaction to a famous victory, or a famous score: 'And they'll be dancing in the streets of [wherever] tonight, I can tell you.'

5   About the end of the game: 'And the referee blows for no side.'

— JUST TWO DECADES AGO —

From the Introduction of the 1984–5 Playfair *Rugby Union Annual*:

'A World Cup competition every four years, along the lines of the Soccer World Cup, has been suggested and has met with considerable support, particularly from the players themselves. However, there is a weighty body of opinion who see Rugby Union as one of the last bastions of amateur sport, whose purpose is to strengthen friendly relations between countries rather than to introduce divisive, competitive feelings into the game.'

— FAMOUS TOUCH JUDGE —

Denis Thatcher, the husband of former British Prime Minister Margaret, was a senior rugby referee who acted as one of the touch judges at the 1956 France v England international in the Stade Colombes, Paris. It is tempting to wonder if Sir Denis ever found Maggie harder to control than a pack of rampaging forwards!

— WELCOME WORCESTER —

Worcester's Sixways Stadium became the 25th Premiership venue when the Warriors began their 2004–5 campaign.

— NAP HAND —

Prop Adrian Olver is the only player to have appeared for five different clubs in the Premiership. His unique collection is Saracens, Bedford, Rotherham, Harlequins and Gloucester.

— BREAKING THE CODE —

Code words are part and parcel of rugby, especially when it comes to line-out calls and back-row moves. The Welsh team of the mid-1970s were no different, but on one occasion a code caused more trouble than it was worth and had to be abandoned – but only after much hilarity.

The Wales team had a pack in which Pontypool's Terry Cobner was on one flank and Swansea's Trevor Evans was on the other. The scrum-half, Gareth Edwards, was instructed to shout out any word beginning with P (for Pontypool) if he was going to launch an attack on Cobner's side of the scrummage, and any word starting with S (for Swansea) if the ball was going to be swung out on Evans's side. However, at the first scrum, Edwards shouted out 'Psychology!' and forwards set off in both directions.

— THE BIRTH OF SEVENS —

Rugby's highly entertaining short-form game, sevens, was invented by the Melrose club in the Scottish Borders in 1883.

— BLASTS FROM THE PAST —

It's fascinating, from the perspective of the early 21st century, to note some of the clubs that have contributed star players to the Lions in past years. Many have fallen upon very harsh times and are nowhere near the force they once were. Worse still, some of them are no longer individual clubs in their own right, having either merged or simply faded away.

The list of clubs is long and includes the likes of Birkenhead Park, Old Leysians, London Scottish, Blackheath, Moseley, Dublin Wanderers, Guy's Hospital, Northern, North of Ireland, Bart's Hospital, Aspatria, Kilmarnock, Percy Park, Penarth, Abertillery, Bradford, Old Millhillians, Redruth, Kendal, Halifax, Old Merchant Taylors, Old Cranleighans, St Andrew's University, Old Birkonians, Bective Rangers, Somerset Police, Penryn, Maesteg, Dunfermline, Aberdeen University and Metropolitan Police. Many do still exist but enjoy nothing like the elevated status that once marked them out as among the finest clubs in their land.

— JONNY'S HEROES —

Jonny Wilkinson has admitted to having had four sporting heroes as a youngster: Walter Payton, Michael Jordan, Boris Becker and Ellery Hanley.

— MORE CLUBS —

The years 1861 to 1879 witnessed the rapid growth of rugby clubs throughout the whole of the British Isles. Among those founded in this era were Richmond (1861), Sale (1861), West of Scotland (1865), Harlequins (1866), Wasps (1867), Neath (1871), Lansdowne (1872), Llanelli (1872), Dungannon (1873) and Swansea (1874).

— EARLIEST BATH —

New Zealand's Cyril Brownlie became the first player to be sent off in international rugby when, during the All Blacks' 17–11 win over England at Twickenham in 1925, he was dismissed by Welsh referee Albert Freethy for kicking an opponent.

— BILL'S MAD DASH —

English lock-forward Bill Beaumont experienced an extraordinary start to his 1977 Lions tour. He was called out to New Zealand as a replacement, but on the morning of his departure he got caught up in a huge traffic jam *en route* to London's Heathrow Airport. Nothing was moving, and Beaumont realised that his only hope of catching the plane was to leg it the last mile or two into the airport terminal, which he did, carrying all his bags on his shoulders. However, if he'd known what sort of disappointing tour he was joining, he might not have been quite so keen to get there!

— NO BITING —

Welsh hooker Brian Rees was once felled by a punch from an opponent. Regaining his feet, he demanded to know what he had been struck for. 'Biting,' said the player who had floored him, showing Rees a full set of teeth marks on his body. Without saying another word, Rees merely grinned broadly to reveal a large toothless gap where his front teeth would have been. To his credit, the opponent immediately apologised.

— NIL POINTS —

England have four times drawn a match 0–0. The first occasion was in 1910, against Ireland, in the second match ever played at Twickenham, and the others were in 1930, against Scotland, in 1962, against Wales, and in 1963, against Ireland.

— MORE UNIONS —

The Scottish Rugby Union was formed in 1873, the Irish Rugby Union in 1879 and the Welsh Rugby Union in 1881. The French Rugby Federation did not exist until 1920.

— PACKING THEM IN —

More than 5 million spectators have attended Heineken Cup matches since the European club competition was launched in 1995–6.

— TOP 20 INTERNATIONAL TRY SCORERS* —

1	David Campese (Australia)	64 (101 matches)
2	Rory Underwood (England)	49 (85)
3	Christian Cullen (New Zealand)	46 (58)
4	Daisuke Ohata (Japan)	45 (51)
5	Jeff Wilson (New Zealand)	44 (60)
6	Joost van der Westhuizen (South Africa)	38 (89)
	Serge Blanco (France)	38 (93)
8	Jonah Lomu (New Zealand)	37 (63)
9	John Kirwan (New Zealand)	35 (63)
10	Doug Howlett (New Zealand)	34 (45)
	Gareth Thomas (Wales)	34 (80)
12	Ieuan Evans (Wales)	33 (72)
13	Philippe Saint-Andre (France)	32 (69)
14	Brian Lima (Samoa)	31 (59)
	Will Greenwood (England)	31 (55)
16	Joe Roff (Australia)	30 (86)
	Tim Horan (Australia)	30 (80)
	Philippe Sella (France)	30 (111)
	Jeremy Guscott (England)	30 (65)
	Tana Umaga (New Zealand)	30 (62)

As at 1 January 2005

— WHAT GARETH WAS THINKING —

When he scored his famous try for the Barbarians against the All Blacks at Cardiff Arms Park in 1973, what exactly went through Gareth Edwards' mind? In his book *Gareth Edwards: The Autobiography* (Headline, 1999), Edwards writes, 'When I caught the ball, it was almost like an interception because I knew John Bevan was waiting outside me and Joe Karam was sizing him up. So I shouted to Derek Quinnell in Welsh, "Throw it here." I still remember the surge of adrenalin as I took the pass and hit the gain line before sweeping around Karam.

'What do you think about in those split seconds? Was I contemplating a glorious touchdown at the end of a superb movement? No, not at all. The only thing in my mind was whether my hamstrings would stand up to the all-out sprinting

I was now doing. I prayed they wouldn't seize up in that mad dash for the corner. Whether there was time for me to run the last few yards to the line, I wouldn't know even now.

'The reason I dived was that I remembered something Bill Samuel had taught me at school. Bill said that when you dive for the line, it makes it more difficult for the defending side to stop you. I knew the cover was coming across and was closing me down fast, but I was too scared to look to see just how close they were. In the event, of course, I think it was Grant Batty who managed to collar me, but my momentum was enough to get me there.'

— TRAGIC FIRST TOUR —

RL Seddon, England's captain for the inaugural tour of Australia and New Zealand in 1888, was drowned in a boating accident in Australia. Andrew Stoddart, who also led England at cricket, took over the captaincy.

— BATH HEROES —

The Bath team that became the first English winners of the Heineken Cup on 31 January 1998 was coached by Andy Robinson, now in charge of England. The team's line-up comprised Jonathan Callard, Ieuan Evans, Phil de Glanville, Jeremy Guscott, Adedayo Adebayo, Mike Catt, Andy Nicol (captain), Dave Hilton, Mark Regan (rep Federico Mendez, 78), Victor Ubogu, Martin Haag, Nigel Redman, Nathan Thomas (rep Russell Earnshaw, 71), Richard Webster, Dan Lyle.

Full back Callard scored all of Bath's points in a tense 19–18 win against Brive in Bordeaux, including the conversion of his own try and a last-gasp penalty – his fourth of the game.

— RUGBY BARD —

Scrum-half Gareth Edwards was ordained into the Gorsedd of Welsh Bards in 1976, with the Druid of Wales, the Reverend Bryn Williams, somewhat strangely introducing him to the Inner Circle of the Royal National Eisteddfod as 'the wizard of the round ball'.

— THE BOY CARDIFF —

In the 1991 World Cup, a Western Samoan centre called To'o Vaega scored a try that helped his country to a famous victory against Wales in Cardiff. To commemorate this win, and his own part in it, Vaega later named his newborn son Cardiff. Disgruntled at seeing their once-proud nation humbled by the fierce-tackling South Sea Islanders, Welsh fans attempted to disguise their pain by joking – with more than a pinch of black humour – that it was a good job their team had not being playing against the whole of Samoa.

— THE ONE THAT GOT AWAY —

The late Colin Elsey was a specialist rugby photographer who took some of the most memorable pictures of the last 30 years, the iconic image of giant English prop Fran Cotton caked in mud during the 1977 British Lions tour of New Zealand being just one example.

But Elsey was always haunted by his failure to capture Gareth Edwards' famous try for the Barbarians against the All Blacks at Cardiff in 1973. 'I had been in the perfect position at the Taff End,' he once said, 'but the All Blacks started to dominate and I moved towards the other end of the pitch. Just as I was doing so, Phil Bennett started to counter-attack from close to the Barbarians' end. I got two or three shots as they came past me down the touchline, but then Gareth went and dived right into the corner of the ground I had just left! I have since been asked if I have a picture of that try more than anything else, and it still hurts to admit that I missed it!'

— CELTIC ANTHEMS —

THE FLOWER OF SCOTLAND

O Flower of Scotland
When will we see your like again
That fought and died for
Your wee bit hill and glen
And stood against him
Proud Edward's army
And set him homeward
Tae think again

★

Those days are passed now
And in the past they must remain
But we can still rise now
And be the nation again
That stood against him
Proud Edward's army
And sent him homeward
Tae think again

IRELAND'S CALL

Come the day
And come the hour
Come the power and the glory
We have come to answer
Our country's call
From the four proud provinces of Ireland

Ireland, Ireland
Together standing tall
Shoulder to shoulder
We'll answer Ireland's call

Ireland, Ireland
Together standing tall
Shoulder to shoulder
We'll answer Ireland's call

HEN WLAD FY NHADAU

Mae hen wlad fy nhadau yn annwyl if mi
Gwlad beirdd a chantorion, enwogion o fri
Ei gwrol ryfelwyr, gwlad garwyr tra mad
Dros ryddid collasant ein gwaed

Gwlad, gwlad, pleidiol wyf i'm gwlad
Tre mor yn fur i'r bur hoff bau
O gydded i'r heniaith bar hau

Gwlad, gwlad, etc

— ACKERMAN'S WOE —

On the 1983 British Lions tour of New Zealand, things didn't go well from the start. The side lost their second match, to Auckland, and even at that early stage they were suffering some of the serious injuries that were to bedevil the entire tour.

The first Test, in Christchurch against the All Blacks, was seen as the key moment of the tour. The opening game should favour the tourists, for the Lions team had had time to work on formations and to come together as a side. The All Blacks would inevitably be rustier, but likely to improve as the series developed.

The Lions led 9–6 at half-time and had a wonderful opportunity to score a crucial try, but alas the Welsh centre, Rob Ackerman of London Welsh and Wales, chose to go on his own a few yards from the New Zealand try line and was held up. Outside him, he had a man free awaiting a certain try-scoring pass, had it come.

The Lions lost that Test 16–12, and the mood was grim that night in the team hotel in the city. England wing John Carleton, who hadn't played that day, said at one stage of the night, 'We lost today, and we'll lose this Test series 4–0. I'm telling you that now.'

Carleton was proved 100 per cent correct as the Lions tumbled to a 4–0 Test-match whitewash against the rampant New Zealanders. They went down 9–0 in the second Test at Wellington, 15–8 in the third Test at Dunedin and, finally, a thumping 38–6 in the last game of the tour, at Eden Park, Auckland. It was a bitter outcome for Ciaran Fitzgerald's men, who had set out on their 18-match tour with such high hopes.

The truth was that the Lions side of 1983 simply wasn't good enough. They lacked the star material of their great predecessors of 1971 and 1974, particularly players like Welshmen Gareth Edwards, JPR Williams, JJ Williams, Barry John, Phil Bennett, Gerald Davies and others, such as Irish midfield genius Mike Gibson and brilliant Scot Andy Irvine. Nor did the team contain forwards of the quality of Mervyn Davies, Willie John McBride, Gordon Brown, Fergus Slattery, Fran Cotton, Roger Uttley, Peter Dixon and Derek Quinnell.

— OLYMPIC CHAMPIONS —

The United States of America are the reigning Olympic rugby champions, having beaten France 17–3 in Paris in 1924, the last time the game was included in an Olympic Games. The Americans also won gold in the Antwerp Games of 1920, again beating France – the only other team that entered – in the final.

The only other two Olympic rugby titles went to France in 1900 (they beat Germany in Paris) and Australia at London in 1908. Australia were represented by their national side, as the Wallabies were at that time making their first tour of Britain, while their Olympic final opponents were England – or, rather, the Cornwall team, who had just won the county championship!

— THE GOSPEL ACCORDING TO SIR CLIVE —

'We won the World Cup because we did 100 things 1 per cent better than everyone else.'
– *Sir Clive Woodward, England coach 1997–2004*

— HYWL —

The way in which the Welsh play rugby is often described by the use of just one Welsh word: *hywl*. It is a word that has many meanings, taking in 'passion', 'enjoyment' and 'having fun'. But, in this case, there really is no need for a translation. *Hywl* sums it up.

— IN THE BLOOD —

Derek Quinnell, the former Wales and British Lions forward, is often referred to as the head of a rugby dynasty that has also produced another Lion in his son Scott Quinnell and a third Welsh international in Scott's brother Craig. What is not widely known (outside of Wales, anyway) is that Derek's wife, Medora, might just have something to do with it, too; she is the younger sister of Barry John, the legendary Welsh and British Isles fly-half.

— SIR TASKER WATKINS —

On 16 August 1944, on the killing fields around Falaise in Normandy, Major Tasker Watkins of the 53rd Welsh Division performed a prolonged act of gallantry that was to earn him the Victoria Cross, Britain's highest military honour. The following text comprises the official citation recording the actions of a man who played for and became president of his club, Glamorgan Wanderers; had a distinguished legal career; and then, in 1993 – as Sir Tasker Watkins VC, GBE, DL – was elected as president of the Welsh Rugby Union:

'In northwest Europe, on the evening of 16 August 1944, Major Watkins was commanding a company of the Welsh Regiment. The battalion was ordered to attack objectives near the railway at Bafour. Major Watkins' company had to cross open cornfields in which booby-traps had been set. It was not yet dusk and the company soon came under heavy machine-gun fire from posts in the corn and farther back, and also fire from an 88mm gun; many casualties were caused and the advance was slowed up.

'Major Watkins, the only officer left, placed himself at the head of his men and under short-range fire charged two posts in succession, personally killing or wounding the occupants with his Sten gun. On reaching his objective, he found an anti-tank gun manned by a German soldier; his Sten gun jammed, so he threw it in the German's face and shot him with his pistol before he had time to recover.

'Major Watkins' company now had only some 30 men left and was counter-attacked by 50 enemy infantry. Major Watkins directed the fire of his men and then led a bayonet charge, which resulted in the almost complete destruction of the enemy.

'It was now dusk and orders were given for the battalion to withdraw. These orders were not received by Major Watkins' company, as the wireless set had been destroyed. They now found themselves alone and surrounded in depleted numbers and in failing light. Major Watkins decided to rejoin his battalion by passing round the flank of the enemy position he had advanced upon, but while passing through the cornfields once more, he was challenged by an enemy post at close range. He ordered his men to scatter and himself charged the post with a Bren gun and silenced it. He then led the remnants of his company back to battalion headquarters. His superb gallantry and total disregard for his own safety during an extremely difficult period were responsible for saving the lives of his men, and had a decisive influence on the course of the battle. The main road to Falaise from the west was effectively cut by his action and was never after used by the enemy.'

— BROTHERS IN ARMS —

It was quite a day for three sets of Irish brothers when Ireland beat Wales 13–10 at Cardiff Arms Park in 1924. Not only could George and Harry Stephenson, Dickie and Billy Collopy and Frank and Tom Hewitt celebrate being together on a winning side, but Frank Hewitt became the youngest Irish player to score an international try, and he and Tom also became the first Irish brothers to score tries in an international game.

— THE WORDS OF THE HAKA —

Ka mate! Ka mate! Ka ora! Ka ora!
(I die! I die! I live! I live!)

Ka mate! Ka mate! Ka ora! Ka ora!
(I die! I die! I live! I live!)

Tenei te tangata puhuru huru
(This is the hairy man)

Nana nei i tiki mai
(Who fetched the Sun)

Whakawhiti te ra
(And caused it to shine again)

A upa...ne! ka upa...ne!
(One upward step! Another upward step!)

A upane kaupane whiti te ra!
(One upward step, another...the Sun shines!)

Hi!

— ENGLAND'S WORLD CUP PARADE —

On Monday 8 December 2003, the England rugby squad paraded the Webb Ellis Cup by open-top bus through central London. More than 750,000 turned out on a bitterly cold winter day to cheer English sport's newest heroes, and rugby union was suddenly in the forefront of popular minds. England's World Cup win had transformed English rugby into a big business.

How the day was organised:

10:30am	England squad meet media at Intercontinental Hotel, Hyde Park Corner, and board buses
Noon	Parade is started by the Lord Mayor of London, Ken Livingstone, at Marble Arch
Noon–1pm	Parade progresses down Oxford Street to Oxford Circus, and then down Regent Street and Haymarket to Trafalgar Square
1pm	Two squad buses arrive on North Terrace of Trafalgar Square. Television and radio interviews
1.20pm	Buses leave under police escort and return to Hotel Intercontinental
1:30pm–2pm	Team members conduct more media interviews and attend RFU reception
2pm	Media leave and squad prepares to meet the Queen
4pm	Squad, support staff and relatives go to Buckingham Palace for tea with the Queen in the Picture Gallery
6:30pm	Number ten Downing Street hosts Prime Minister's champagne reception in the State Rooms
7:30pm	Return to hotel

What they said during the parade:

Martin Johnson (captain): 'It's absolutely mind-blowing. I didn't have any idea what this parade would be like, but it is incredible. It's indescribable. Apart from royal events, I can't think when London's been like that.'

Clive Woodward (head coach): 'The scenes at Manly, at Sydney, at Heathrow, they've all been fantastic, but this is something I don't think any of us were expecting at all. Trafalgar Square packed out summed up the whole thing, but from the moment we started the parade it was incredible. None of us have ever experienced anything like this.'

Phil Vickery (prop forward): 'It doesn't seem right for rugby, does it?'

Woodward (soon to become Sir Clive) again: 'We've got to move things forward now, and that's what I fully intend to do. If it doesn't move forward, you'll know because you'll see it on the pitch. It's a brutal business, and I'm very clear about this: if we take our foot off the pedal and we have a string of losses, there'll be changes, including myself.'

With Johnson and a string of other senior players deciding to retire during the first half of 2004, England went on to lose five of their next eight internationals. Woodward resigned on 2 September 2004.

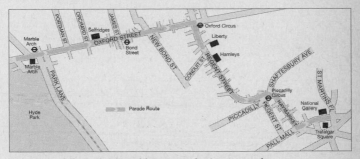

The route of the England World Cup squad's victory parade

— FIRST DEFEAT —

The first team to beat England at Twickenham was South Africa, with the 1913 Springboks winning there 9–3.

— THE FATHER OF WELSH RUGBY —

Rugby has always been worshipped like a religion in Wales. How appropriate, then, that the man who introduced the game to the Principality in 1850 was the Reverend Rowland Williams, of St David's College in Lampeter.

— LIONS LEADERS —

Ireland has provided more captains for the leadership of British Isles sides overseas than any other home country. Since the first tour in 1888 to Australia and New Zealand, eight Irishmen have been chosen as leaders:

- **Tom Smythe** (1910, Malone and Ireland)
- **Sammy Walker** (1938, Instonians and Ireland)
- **Karl Mullen** (1950, Old Belvedere and Ireland)
- **Robin Thompson** (1955, Instonians and Ireland)
- **Ronnie Dawson** (1959, Wanderers and Ireland)
- **Tom Kiernan** (1968, Cork Constitution and Ireland)
- **Willie John McBride** (1974, Ballymena and Ireland)
- **Ciaran Fitzgerald** (1983, St Mary's College, Dublin, and Ireland)

England is the next biggest contributor of Lions captains, and in fact the England team has also earned the honour of having a Lions captain for eight tours. However, only seven Englishmen have been chosen (Leicester's Martin Johnson earned the accolade both in 1997 to South Africa and also in 2001 to Australia). Here's a list of Englishmen to have captained the Lions

- **RL Seddon** (1888, Swinton and Lancashire)
- **J Hammond** (1896, Cambridge University and Blackheath)
- **Rev MM Mullineux** (1899, Blackheath)
- **R Cove-Smith** (1924, Old Merchant Taylors and England)
- **FD Prentice** (1930, Leicester and England)
- **WB Beaumont** (1980, Fylde and England)
- **MO Johnson** (1997, Leicester and England)
- **MO Johnson** (2001, Leicester and England)

At one stage, Ireland provided every Lions captain for a spell of 21 years, stretching from Sammy Walker's 1938 tourists to the 1959 party led by Ronnie Dawson. But, of course, with the War years intervening, there were only four tours in that era.

— ON THE RUN —

Gareth Edwards, the man widely acknowledged to be the best scrum-half who ever lived, played 53 consecutive internationals for Wales between 1967 and 1978.

— TOP CAPS —

Before the 2004–5 season, Bath held the unique record of being the only club to have fielded a full 15-man set of international capped players in a Premiership starting line-up. It happened at the Recreation Ground on 26 September 1998, and Bath beat Gloucester 21–16. Well, they had to, really, didn't they?

— TAKING THE MICK —

When Ulster flanker Gordon Hamilton raced 30 yards to score a dramatic late try at Lansdowne Road in 1991, it seemed as if Australia were about to be dumped out of the World Cup at the quarter-final stage by Ireland. But the home crowd's ecstasy turned to despair when, minutes later and with just 90 seconds left on the clock, Michael Lynagh looped around David Campese to touch down for a thrilling, and truly match-winning, try of his own at the end of a magnificent last-ditch Wallaby attack. Fly-half Lynagh's grandmother was born in Ballinrobe in County Mayo.

— WHAT THE DEUCE? —

Welsh rugby legend JPR Williams won sporting fame initially in tennis. In 1966, three years before being first capped as full back by Wales, he became Wimbledon Junior Champion. He returned briefly to tennis in 1970, reaching the final of the British National Under-21s Championships. JPR also played violin in the Welsh National Youth Orchestra.

— 15 A SIDE —

International teams were not reduced from 20 to 15 until 1877, two years after England won their first meeting with Ireland. The Irish were beaten at the Oval, London, by one goal, one dropped goal and one try to nil. In 1881, when England played Wales for the first time, they thrashed them at Blackheath by seven goals, one dropped goal and six tries to nil.

— IT HIT THE POST AND CAME OUT —

There are plenty of hard-luck stories, in rugby and in soccer, about great shots or great kicks that hit the post – or the bar – when they look for all the world to have gone in or over for a match-clinching score. But nothing, perhaps, comes close to the tale of England wing Hal Sever.

In the dying minutes of the 1938 International Championship decider at Twickenham, with England attacking desperately to overturn a Scotland lead of 18–16, Sever – put through for what surely would otherwise have been the winning try – for some reason cut back inside the remaining cover rather than continue to run into the space that had opened up on the outside. The result was that he ran smack bang into one of the goalposts and, in the impact, spilled the ball. Scottish hands eagerly scooped up the loose ball and, in a breakaway movement, the visitors eventually touched down at the other end for the try that actually did clinch the game.

— TV GAME —

The 1938 international between England and Scotland at Twickenham was the first to be televised live.

— THE SUBMARINE LION —

When the squad was announced for the 1955 British Lions party to tour South Africa, it was revealed that three scrum-halves had been included: the Englishmen Dickie Jeeps and Johnny Williams, plus Trevor Lloyd of Maesteg and Wales.

Lloyd was easily the oldest and much the most interesting of the three. He had served on submarines as a 17-year-old off the Malay Peninsula during the Second World War, tracking the movements of Japanese cruisers and supporting British spies who were being dropped off on the islands at night.

On the Lions tour, however, Lloyd didn't make a great impact, and didn't play in a Test match. But he faced the disappointment with the natural philosophical air of a man who had seen many men die in hostile waters during the War. Lloyd knew that there were more important things in life than a rugby tour.

— HOW IT BEGAN: GEORGIA —

Jacques Hespekian, a Frenchman of Armenian descent who moved to the Georgian capital, Tbilisi, in 1956, is credited with the introduction of rugby union to the country. Hespekian found that Georgians soon took to the sport, thanks to the popularity of their traditional and aggressive football game called *Lelo*, which was originally derived from a medieval warrior-training discipline.

— FIRST BRITISH ISLES TOURISTS —

In 1888, the first British Isles team to tour Australia and New Zealand contained five players from Swinton, three from Salford and one each from Batley, Runcorn, Rochdale Hornets, Bramley, Halifax and Dewsbury. There wasn't a Leicester Tiger, Northampton Saint, Wasp or Harlequin in sight.

— SAMOAN ALL BLACKS —

Critics have often accused New Zealand of cherry-picking the best available talent from the Polynesian populations of the Pacific. Jonah Lomu, for instance, is of Tongan stock and birth, while many Pacific Islanders have actually represented both the All Blacks and the countries of their birth or heritage. Frank Bunce, who helped to inspire the 1991 Western Samoans at the World Cup, later won himself even more of a fearsome reputation as a New Zealand centre. Va'aiga Tuigamala, the powerful wing who for a time in the late 1980s and early 1990s was the most potent attacking weapon in the global game, later switched from the All Blacks and represented Samoa at the 1995 World Cup. Whatever the rights and wrongs, it is a moot point that, at any stage of the last 20 years, the island of Samoa would have been up there with all the very best rugby nations of the world if their selectors had been able or empowered to choose their national XV from every leading player with Samoan blood in his veins.

— ALL-ROUNDERS —

Jeff Wilson and Brian McKechnie have both represented New Zealand at rugby and cricket, although in the latter sport both only played in one-day internationals, not fully-fledged Test matches.

— GREAT TRIES 1 —

GARETH EDWARDS
BARBARIANS v NEW ZEALAND
CARDIFF ARMS PARK, 1973

1   A long cross-kick ahead by All Black wing Bryan Williams, in just the second minute of this famous match, is chased by Phil Bennett, the Barbarians fly-half. An awkwardly bouncing ball is gathered up by the Welshman, with his back to the opposition and deep inside his own 25. New Zealand flanker Alistair Scown is the first All Black to get to Bennett, but his would-be flying tackle is evaded as the fly-half turns sharply to his left. Now facing forward, and facing a line of New Zealanders preparing to tackle him, Bennett throws two opponents off balance with two wonderfully exaggerated sidesteps, which take him left and back across and in front of the Barbarians posts. With a third All Black about to tackle him, Bennett offloads to JPR Williams, the great Welsh full back, who has come close to lend support.

2   Almost as soon as he receives Bennett's pass, JPR is collared unceremoniously by his namesake, Bryan Williams, who has followed up his original kick to play his team-mates onside. Now, coming infield to try to snuff out the Baa-baas' attack at source, he grabs JPR around the neck and forces him to offload in turn to John Pullin.

3   Pullin, the Bristol and England hooker, is perhaps the great unsung hero of this celebrated score. Swiftly sizing up the situation in a manner that would have done credit to some of the best half backs of his generation, he straightens the movement and, in effect, makes the key decision to continue the counter-attack. Gareth Edwards is momentarily alongside him, as he tries to get himself onside, but Pullin strides forward past the scrum-half and, after gaining 15 yards of territory, passes outside him to John Dawes.

4   Dawes, the great Welsh centre, quickens the attack with a burst of acceleration that takes him away from his own 25-yard line and almost to halfway. He swerves inside one All Black opponent, draws another and, as he is tackled, passes inside him to the supporting Tom David.

5   Wales flanker David charges on over the halfway line and into the heart of the spread-out New Zealand cover. Tackled, he skilfully keeps the ball away from his opponent by holding it in his right hand and, as he falls, slinging it back inside him towards the touchline.

6   'Brilliant by Quinnell!' yells Cliff Morgan, up in the BBC TV commentary box, and the legendary former Welsh fly-half is spot on. Grizzled Wales utility forward Derek Quinnell stoops on the run to pick up David's flung pass at shin level and – staggering to stay on his feet as he holds on grimly to the ball – looks to his left instinctively for support.

7   Quinnell tosses a right-handed flip pass towards John Bevan, on the left wing. But, as he does so, Edwards races up inside Bevan and takes the ball at full tilt. All Black full back Joe Karam, clearly seeing Bevan as the original target of Quinnell's pass, is wrong-footed and Edwards hares across in front of Bevan and around Karam's despairing tackle. Almost on the touchline, as he brushes past Karam, Edwards is now up to the New Zealand 25 and clear. Sprinting down the line, he dives for the corner and just manages to beat a last-ditch cover tackle by Grant Batty, who himself has charged across the field from his own left-wing station. 'What a score!' shouts Morgan with classic understatement in a classic moment.

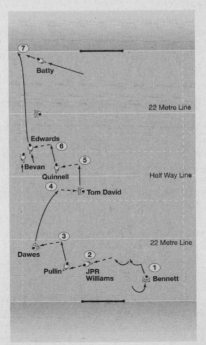

— THE FIRST CLUB —

The first rugby club was formed at Cambridge, in 1839, by Old Rugbeian Arthur Pell, and the game's first set of rules were drawn up at Rugby School in 1845.

— TROUBLE AND STRIFE —

Keen amateur player Tony Piersall was faced with a big problem when his wife kept suggesting that he gave up rugby and concentrated on doing the shopping and the gardening on a Saturday afternoon. He was getting too old for rugby, she insisted. No, commanded. So Tony, a double-glazing salesman in Kent, said he would quit. Then, however, he suddenly started to get a lot of business coming in every Saturday. 'Sorry,' he would say. 'Work again!'

His wife began to get suspicious. She looked in the local paper, but there was no sign of his name in the rugby team he had left behind. Someone called Tony Williams was playing in his place. But when her husband kept having to work each and every Saturday, she became even more suspicious. She called in at the Canterbury Rugby Club. 'Everyone ran for cover, Tony included,' laughed club official David Hay. 'He had been playing under the name of Tony Williams for weeks.'

The morale of this story? Well, he is still married, and now turns out for the Veterans XV. It's called the true spirit of rugby.

— YOUNGEST TO BE HONOURED —

In January 2003, Jonny Wilkinson became the youngest rugby player ever to receive a New Year's honour when he was awarded the MBE for his services to the game.

— UNLUCKY 13 —

When the first Wales XV gathered in London in 1881 to prepare to take on England at Blackheath in the inaugural international between the two countries, officials discovered that in fact it was a XIII. Two invitations had not reached their destinations, and so the Welsh team was made up to the correct number by the hurried selection of two university students with Wales qualifications.

— BROTHER v BROTHER —

There have been three recent instances of brothers playing against each other at Test level. In the 1999 World Cup, there was the strange sight of Graeme and Steve Bachop – who had played together four times for New Zealand – lining up in the colours of Japan and Samoa respectively. Earlier in the year, Mike and Tana Umaga played for Samoa and New Zealand, respectively, in an international at Albany, while in 2000 Pita Alatini represented New Zealand at fly-half and found himself in direct opposition to his brother Sam in a match against Tonga.

— THE WOODWARD ERA —

Sir Clive Woodward was in charge of England's rugby team from 15 November 1997, when they drew 15–15 against Australia at Twickenham, and he retired less than two months after his final match, when a tired and weakened side lost 51-15 to the Wallabies in Brisbane on 26 June 2004. His overall playing record was: played 82, won 59, drew 2 and lost 22. The zenith of his stewardship was the extraordinary run of success that began in March 2002, just after England had lost to France in Paris, and he took Martin Johnson's team right up to the winning of the World Cup on 22 November 2003.

In that time, England played 23 internationals and lost just once – when a second-string side were beaten 17–16 by France in Marseilles during the warm-up period that preceded the departure to Australia for the World Cup campaign.

— CHANGING TIMES —

Of the nine clubs that contested England's first six National Cup (now called the Powergen Cup) competitions from 1972 to 1977, only two remain in the country's elite. Gloucester won the inaugural cup in 1972, and Gosforth (who have now become Newcastle Falcons) won in both 1976 and 1977, but all the other teams who featured in those first six finals – Moseley, Coventry, Bristol, London Scottish, Bedford, Rosslyn Park and Waterloo – currently exist outside the English Premiership.

— THE FIRST LEAGUES —

In 1987–8 the Rugby Football Union launched its first official league structure in England. It is fascinating, in light of the way the game has since been transformed by professionalism, to study the make-up of Divisions 1, 2 and 3 in that inaugural season of what was then called Courage League rugby. In order of how they finished, they were as follows:

NATIONAL ONE

Leicester (champions)
Wasps
Harlequins
Bath
Gloucester
Orrell
Moseley
Nottingham
Bristol
Waterloo
Coventry (relegated)
Sale (relegated)

NATIONAL TWO

Rosslyn Park (promoted)
Liverpool St Helens (promoted)
Saracens
Headingley
Bedford
Richmond
London Scottish
London Irish
London Welsh
Gosforth
Blackheath
Northampton (relegated)

NATIONAL THREE

Wakefield (promoted)
West Hartlepool
Plymouth

Sheffield
Vale of Lune
Fylde,
Metropolitan Police
Maidstone
Exeter
Nuneaton
Morley (relegated)
Birmingham (relegated).

In 1987–8, Worcester finished fourth from bottom in Midlands 2 (West) – in effect, the sixth tier down the new league ladder.

JONNY WILKINSON: FROM DEBUTANT TO — WORLD CUP WINNER —

England's Jonny Wilkinson made his international debut on 4 April 1998, coming on as a replacement for Mike Catt against Ireland. His 52nd cap was in the World Cup final against Australia on 22 November 2003. His last-minute, extra-time drop goal, which effectively decided the game, took his international points tally to 817 – an average of 15.6 per game over those 52 appearances. In his first 25 Five and Six Nations matches between 1998 and 2003, Wilkinson scored 379 points, at an average of 15.16 per game.

— TOP 10 MOST INTERNATIONAL PENALTIES* —

1	Neil Jenkins (Wales)	235 (87 matches)
2	Diego Dominguez (Italy)	208 (74)
3	Andrew Mehrtens (New Zealand)	186 (70)
4	Michael Lynagh (Australia)	177 (72)
5	Matthew Burke (Australia)	174 (81)
6	Jonny Wilkinson (England)	161 (52)
7	Gavin Hastings (Scotland)	140 (61)
8	Grant Fox (New Zealand)	128 (46)
9	Nicky Little (Fiji)	120 (53)
10	Gareth Rees (Canada)	110 (55)

* As at 1 January 2005

— ALIVE —

Rugby, and Uruguayan rugby in particular, will forever be linked with the extraordinary story of what happened in the aftermath of a 1972 plane crash in the snow-covered Andes mountains. The feature film *Alive* has immortalised the terrible choice which faced those who survived the crash: to eat or not to eat the flesh of dead colleagues and relatives in a desperate attempt to stay alive during the three months that passed before those who remained were rescued by Chilean mountaineers.

Of the 45 passengers who boarded the doomed flight from Montevideo to Santiago on 13 October 1972, more than half were rugby players from the Old Christians club or youth players from the same club. The rest were members of their families or supporters. Some died in the crash, while ten others perished in an avalanche sometime later. Others who did not make it included those who could not bring themselves to eat human flesh to survive.

Ultimately, 16 people survived, among them Gustavo Zerbino, then aged 17 and someone who was to go on to play senior international rugby for Uruguay. 'After we were rescued, we were told that it was impossible that we could have survived in those conditions,' he said recently. 'But perhaps the fact that we were so naive was a bonus. We didn't know anything about survival in the mountains, and that may actually have saved our lives. Experienced mountaineers were saying they could not believe how we survived, but we were tested to the full and we proved them wrong. It is difficult to say what kept us alive, other than our unerring faith, our will to live and, of course, God's will. We were just a bunch of teenagers with little or no life experience. But there is very little doubt that the fact that we were school mates, that we trusted each other, that we were committed Christians, and that we played rugby together helped.'

Zerbino was one of six rugby players who survived, the others being Roberto Cannessa, Roy Harley, Fernando Parrado, Antonio Visentin and Alvaro Mangino. Only Mangino, whose leg was shattered during the crash, never played again; indeed, within three months of being rescued, the other five were all back on a rugby field. 'After the tragedy and our miraculous escape, it was rugby which again helped us, by allowing us to keep our sanity and regain a sense of being and purpose,' added Zerbino. 'Rugby played a significant part in our survival, but it became even more important afterwards as we tried to rebuild our lives.

'The night after we were found, a helicopter lifted out eight of our party. I remained in the eight who stayed behind for a while, with three of the Chilean mountaineers who had rescued us. None of us slept that night. The Chileans were very good people, and they said that we shouldn't tell of what happened to us, and they were trying to protect us. But we had to tell the truth, because we owed that much to our dead friends and families. We were the first human beings prepared to acknowledge that we survived that way. And, as far as rugby was concerned, it acted as a therapy afterwards. We played because we wanted to make other people and ourselves believe that the future was more important than what had happened up in the mountains. There was incredible passion, and we trained every day and played as if our lives depended on it. We played each game as if it was our last – in memory of our dead friends.'

In the 14 years that followed the crash, the Old Christians club won the Uruguayan championship 12 times.

— GRAND SLAM TEAM BROKEN BY WAR —

England's International Championship-winning squad of 1914 saw seven of its members killed in the First World War. The captain, the handsome and talented Ronnie Poulton, died at the hands of a German sniper in May 1915, and Arthur Harrison was posthumously awarded the Victoria Cross for his courageous part in the April 1918 raid on a U-boat base at Zeebrugge. Harrison, the only England international to be awarded a VC, had won his only two caps during the 1914 championship, which featured victories against Wales (10-9), Ireland (17-12), Scotland (16-15) and France (39-13), and which in modern times would have been fêted as a Grand Slam.

— ENGLAND'S WOE —

In the 1991 World Cup final at Twickenham, which England lost 12–6 to Australia despite enjoying the lion's share of possession, fly-half Rob Andrew received the ball 41 times, running it on 26 occasions. Andrew's opposite number Michael Lynagh, however, received the ball just 17 times from inside him, and passed it on to his backs a mere four times. Boring, boring Australia? As the Aussies would say, just look at the name on 'Bill' (the nickname the Australian players later gave to the World Cup trophy, the Webb Ellis Cup).

— FIVE/SIX NATIONS TOURNAMENT WINNERS —

The RBS Six Nations Championship – previously known as the Five Nations Championship and, before that, for many years merely as the International Championship – reached a zenith in 2003 when that year's champions, England, were also crowned seven months later as World Cup winners. For perhaps the first time in a century, it was the northern hemisphere – with its main 'shop window', the Six Nations Championship – which could boast possession of the sport's chief assets.

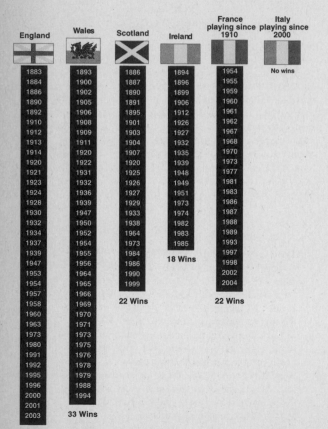

England	Wales	Scotland	Ireland	France playing since 1910	Italy playing since 2000
1883	1893	1886	1894	1954	No wins
1884	1900	1887	1896	1955	
1886	1902	1890	1899	1959	
1890	1905	1891	1906	1960	
1892	1906	1895	1912	1961	
1910	1908	1901	1926	1962	
1912	1909	1903	1927	1967	
1913	1911	1904	1932	1968	
1914	1920	1907	1935	1970	
1920	1922	1920	1939	1973	
1921	1931	1925	1948	1977	
1923	1932	1926	1949	1981	
1924	1936	1927	1951	1983	
1928	1939	1929	1973	1986	
1930	1947	1933	1974	1987	
1932	1950	1938	1982	1988	
1934	1952	1964	1983	1989	
1937	1954	1973	1985	1993	
1939	1955	1984	**18 Wins**	1997	
1947	1956	1986		1998	
1953	1964	1990		2002	
1954	1965	1999		2004	
1957	1966	**22 Wins**		**22 Wins**	
1958	1969				
1960	1970				
1963	1971				
1973	1973				
1980	1975				
1991	1976				
1992	1978				
1995	1979				
1996	1988				
2000	1994				
2001	**33 Wins**				
2003					
35 Wins					

— CAN'T GET NO SATISFACTION —

'I wasn't satisfied with the World Cup victory. I don't think we played very well in the tournament. We've been very narrow in our approach for the last two years.'

– Andy Robinson, England head coach,
before his first match in charge in
November 2004.

— TOUR FROM HELL —

In June 1998, at the end of his first year in charge of England, Clive Woodward took a severely weakened squad on a summer tour of the southern hemisphere which has since taken on an almost mythical importance in terms of the subsequent achievements of his team. Jonny Wilkinson, Phil Vickery, Josh Lewsey and Matt Dawson all became World Cup winners five and a half years later, and they attribute much of their instructional early international rugby experience to what has entered popular folklore as England's 'tour from hell'. For the record, England lost by a record 76–0 to Australia (Wilkinson's first full cap), 64–22 and 40–10 to New Zealand, and 18–0 to South Africa.

— THE POWER OF TELEVISION —

The inaugural rugby World Cup in 1987 was watched by a worldwide television audience of a mere 300 million people. In the 1991 tournament, the audience had climbed to 1.6 billion, and by 1995 it was 2.67 billion. The 1999 World Cup attracted 3.1 billion viewers, and the 2003 event 3.3 billion in 120 countries. In England, early on the morning of Saturday 22 November 2003, more than 15 million people watched Martin Johnson's team beat Australia to win the World Cup. At the same time, the RAC calculated that there were 10 million fewer cars on the roads of the United Kingdom than was usual for that time on a Saturday.

— WHAT THE CAPTAINS SAID —

There are to date just five men who have led their country to World Cup victory. This is what they said:

1987   DAVID KIRK (NEW ZEALAND): 'The first World Cup was very important to us because, in some way, we were representing all those great New Zealand teams that had gone before. We were the inheritors of a great tradition. It was fantastic to win; there's nothing to compare with it. There was also a lot of relief, as there had been a lot of pressure on us. We were at home and the country had invested a lot of emotional energy in seeing this team win. We had taken our opportunity to be the best in the world and delivered.'

1991   NICK FARR-JONES (AUSTRALIA): 'I can honestly say that the last four minutes of our quarter-final against Ireland at Lansdowne Road were the most emotional of my life, and that includes the birth of my four children. Having been injured after 20 minutes, I was watching from the stands as Gordon Hamilton scored that Irish try. I figured that was the end of my career – two World Cups and twice knocked out. Then Michael Lynagh called the move that led to him scoring the winning try. I can say unashamedly that I burst into tears at the end of it all. After winning the Cup, it wasn't until we got home that we realised how our achievement had captured the imagination of not just die-hard rugby people in Australia, but also those in places like Perth, Adelaide, Hobart and Melbourne.'

1995   FRANÇOIS PIENAAR (SOUTH AFRICA): 'There was a sense of enormity about the whole thing. You had to take a deep breath and take it all in. Black people, coloured people, white people, mixing in the streets and cheering. It hadn't happened before. It was special. On the morning of the final there were four little black kids who sold newspapers around the corner and they were shouting the names of all the players. I'll never forget that. It was a very close final, but we won through Joel Stransky's dropped goal. There was such emotion. When I was presented with the Cup by President Mandela, and when he shook my hand and said "Thank you for what you have done for the country", I said, "No, you've got it wrong. It's what *you* have done that has made the difference." There was this guy incarcerated in jail for 27 years and he came out and wore a Springbok jersey. I maintain that any other President in the world would have had his best suit on, yet he had a white man's shirt on, which was just phenomenal. That's why I said victory wasn't just for the 65,000 crowd in Ellis Park, but for the entire nation of 43 million people.'

1999 JOHN EALES (AUSTRALIA): 'We went into the tournament pretty relaxed. We played up to the fact that we were being overlooked. New Zealand arrived in a black jumbo jet with a mural of the silver fern painted on it. How much more attention could you draw to yourselves? Before the final, we were just so conscious of the opportunity that we had, and that for many of the guys it would be their one and only opportunity to be crowned world champions.'

2003 MARTIN JOHNSON (ENGLAND): 'I'm just happy for the players because they've put so much into it. They put their hearts and souls into this campaign. We were frustrated in the second half, but we have to give credit: Australia are a very good team. With 20 minutes of extra time, it could have gone either way. It couldn't have been closer, and I'm just happy to be on the right side.'

— FIVE-POINTER —

The first international scorer of the five-point try (the value of which was upgraded from four in 1992) was Va'aiga Tuigamala, for New Zealand, against Australia.

— THE LINE-OUT MATCH —

There were no fewer than 111 line-outs in the 1963 International Championship match between Scotland and Wales at Murrayfield, and all because Welsh captain Clive Rowlands felt – quite accurately as it turned out – that playing continually to his forward strength was the best way to win the game. In those days, of course, direct kicks to touch did not have to be from within the 25-yard line, so Rowlands decided to play it tight. It did not help the spectators that the match was also played in heavy rain and occasional sleet, but Wales didn't care about the lack of spectacle: they won 6–0.

— MURRAYFIELD —

Scotland's main rugby stadium was built on land purchased from the Edinburgh Polo Club for £3,800 and hosted its first international in 1925, the Scots celebrating by beating England 14–11. In 1975, a crowd of 104,000 crammed the stadium to see Scotland beat championship winners Wales 12–10, but rebuilding from 1991 to 1994 was required to transform it into today's all-seater stadium holding almost 70,000.

— NO SUNDAYS —

Legendary All Black flanker Michael Jones refused to play rugby on a Sunday, a decision that led to him missing some very important New Zealand games. He said later, 'I didn't want rugby to become a priority over the part of my life that was to continue to honour God. So, despite the fact that it has caused some difficult times, I still feel very assured that they were the right decisions to take, as far as living my life out.'

— ALLEZ FRANCE —

France were admitted to the International Championship (which later became known as the Five Nations Championship) in 1910. In the following year, they gained their first senior international victory by beating Scotland 16–15 in Paris. France did not become sole winners of the Five Nations title until 1959.

— PRIDE OF THE SAMOANS —

Bryan Williams, the great winger and first Samoan to wear the All Black jersey of New Zealand, was coach of Western Samoa when they announced themselves to the World Cup audience by beating Wales 16-13 in Cardiff and reaching the quarter-finals of the 1991 tournament. This was a seminal moment in the history of the game, let alone that of Wales, because it was the first time that a nation from outside the IRFB hierarchy had defeated a team representing one of the IRFB members.

— THE NUMBERS GAME —

Rugby shirts were not commonly numbered for identification until 1897. Standard numbering with regard to players' positions, however, was not implemented by the International Board until 1966.

— THE JOHNSON LEGACY —

Martin Johnson's international career details:

- **Born:** 9 March, 1970 in Solihull

- **Junior representative honours:** England Schools, 1987–8
  England Colts, 1988–9
  New Zealand under 21s, 1990
  England under 21s, 1991–2
  England B, 1991–2

- **Debut for Leicester:** 14 February 1989 (v RAF)

- **Debut for England:** 16 January 1993 (v France)

- **Debut for British Lions:** 26 June 1993 (v New Zealand)

- **England appearances (1993–2003):** 84 (won 67, lost 15, drawn 2)

- **England captaincy record (1998–2003):** 39 (won 34, lost 5)

- **British Lions appearances:** 2 in 1993 (v New Zealand)
  3 in 1997 (v South Africa)
  3 in 2001 (v Australia)
  Overall record: won 4, lost 4

- **British Lions captaincy:** 1997 v South Africa (won two, lost one)
  2001 v Australia (won one, lost two)

— AWESOME FOURSOME —

Gareth Rees, the Canada fly-half, was the only player to appear in the first four rugby World Cups, in 1987, 1991, 1995 and 1999.

— THE SECRET OF THE CAULIFLOWER EAR —

They are the badges of honour among the forwards, who pack down in the sweat-stained boilerhouse of the front five, and even more of a tell-tale sign of the owner's chosen sport than a broken nose or a gap where the front teeth used to be. But how is the cauliflower ear actually 'grown'?

What is more accurately called, in medical terminology, a haematoma of the pinna develops when the ear is continually rubbed, hit or kicked so that bleeding is caused between the covering of the external ear and the cartilage. Large haematomas, causing severely swollen ears, require treatment. It is usually possible to evacuate the built-up blood pockets with a syringe or a large-bore needle, although sometimes a sizeable cut is needed. The cleaned-out wound is then protected by a pressure bandage and antibiotics are prescribed to prevent infection.

— SWEET ANTHEM —

England's adopted rugby anthem, 'Swing Low, Sweet Chariot', is a slave runaway song and Negro spiritual written in 1866 by Henry Thacker Burleigh, whose grandfather had been a slave. It was first sung, spontaneously, by the Twickenham crowd in 1988 when Chris Oti scored a hat-trick of tries in a 35–3 trouncing of Ireland.

— BAD BLOOD IN PARIS —

There were stormy scenes following England's heroic 19–10 quarter-final victory over France in a thunderous 1991 World Cup contest of raw confrontation in Paris. Afterwards, Daniel Dubroca, the French coach, laid the accusation of cheating against David Bishop, the New Zealand referee, and it was also alleged that Dubroca assaulted the official in the area outside the dressing rooms. Denying it, Dubroca said, 'I was simply congratulating the referee. I said, "Bravo." If I touched him, it was a fraternal gesture because I know him so well.' Albert Ferrasse, the president of the French Federation, added that Dubroca's English 'was not good enough to abuse the referee seriously'. No official complaint was made, and no further action was taken, but Dubroca resigned from his post shortly after France's bad-tempered exit from the tournament.

— OLDEST OF THE OLD —

Lansdowne Road in Dublin is the world's oldest international rugby ground. The first match held there was Ireland v England, on 4 February 1884.

— LANE'S END OF THE ROAD COMES EARLY —

Cardiff and Wales wing forward Stuart Lane set a record of the most unwanted kind right at the start of the 1980 Lions tour to South Africa, captained by Englishman Bill Beaumont.

Lane was chosen for the tour opener against Eastern Province, and with the game precisely 50 seconds old he tore his knee ligaments and was carried from the field. The injury was diagnosed as serious, and Lane never played again for the Lions, having to be flown home soon after.

That incident set the tone for the rest of the tour. There were so many injuries that a record number of replacements were required – eight in all. The injuries simply kept coming: all four of the Lions' first-choice half backs, for instance, were seriously injured at one time or another.

Gareth Davies, Ollie Campbell, Stuart Lane, Terry Holmes, Colin Patterson, Phil Blakeway, Fran Cotton, David Richards and Mike Slemen were all either injured for lengthy spells or went home early. The replacements called up in their place were Andy Irvine, Paul Dodge, John Robbie, Steve Smith, Tony Ward, Phil Orr, Ian Stephens and Geoff Williams.

— MURDOCH'S SHAME —

Keith Murdoch, the New Zealand front-row forward, was sent home from the All Blacks' 1972/3 tour of Britain for punching a Welsh security guard during a row at a hotel in Wales. But Murdoch got off the plane taking him home in Darwin, in Australia's Northern Territory, and disappeared...for 16 years. He clearly did not want to face up to what might have followed the disgrace of being sent home, and when he was 'discovered' again by an Australian television crew in 1989, he was busy driving a bulldozer on a north Queensland banana farm.

— SOME BASIC RUGBY UNION RULES —

- The ball must not be passed forward.

- The ball cannot be kicked directly into touch from outside the possessing player's own 22m line.

- A player cannot be closer than 5m from the thrower-in at a line-out.

- All players in the line-out must also be within 15m of the thrower-in, at least until the ball leaves the thrower-in's hands.

- The taker of a quick tap penalty, or free kick, cannot be tackled until he has run 10m, unless he is within 10m of the try line (or in-goal line) when he starts off.

- Once a player has indicated to the referee that he is kicking at goal with a penalty, he cannot change his mind.

- Scrummages must start 'square' and all players must be properly bound until the scrum is deemed to be over.

- The ball can legally emerge from a scrummage anywhere other than from either end of the 'tunnel' into which it is initially put by the scrum-half.

- When a player is tackled and goes to ground, he must release the ball immediately. He must then try to get up, or roll away, and cannot touch the ball again or interfere with the continuation of play until he has got back onto his feet. Failure to release the ball results in a penalty for 'holding on'. Failure to roll away, or similarly to interfere with the play, is also penalised.

  A ruck is deemed to be formed when a player is tackled and a loose ball is on the ground. No handling is permitted in the ruck.

- When a player is tackled and held, but stays on his feet, a maul is deemed to be formed around him. The ball can be passed backwards within a maul only if the ball receiver is properly bound to the maul.

- Once in a maul, a player cannot be tackled around the legs. This is considered dangerous play, and penalised.

- A hand-off must be made with a flat, open palm and not a clenched fist.

— THE FIRST 100 —

In 1981, when Cambridge beat Oxford 9–6 at Twickenham in the 100th Varsity Match, the Light Blues went ahead in the series for the first time (by 44–43).

— THE BALL-MAKER —

William Gilbert, a shoemaker in Rugby who was born in 1799 and died in 1877, is the acknowledged maker of the first rugby ball. As the popularity of the new rugby football game spread, so William Gilbert's expertise in ball-making enabled him to become the leader in this field. In fact, it is distinctly possible (though unprovable) that Gilbert made the balls used in both the historic William Webb Ellis match at Rugby School in 1823 and the first rugby international, between England and Scotland, in 1871. William Gilbert rugby balls are still used today in many matches at all levels, but, whereas the modern rugby ball has a distinctive shape, those used in earlier times were rounder and larger, the shape and size being determined by the pig's bladder from which it was made. (Incidentally, bladders had been used since ancient times for 'ball-type' games, but men soon learned how to encase them in leather for special occasions. Otherwise, they were too easily punctured!)

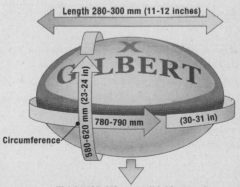

Length 280-300 mm (11-12 inches)

GILBERT

23-24 in

580-620 mm

780-790 mm   (30-31 in)

Circumference

Weight 400-440 grams (14-16 ounces)

— TOP 10 MOST INTERNATIONAL DROP GOALS* —

1	Hugo Porta (Argentina)	25 (57 matches)
2	Rob Andrew (England)	21 (71)
	Jonny Wilkinson (England)	21 (52)
4	Diego Dominguez (Italy)	20 (74)
5	Naas Botha (South Africa)	18 (28)
6	Stefano Bettarello (Italy)	17 (55)
7	Jean-Patrick Lescarboura (France)	15 (28)
8	Jonathan Davies (Wales)	13 (32)
9	Pierre Albaladejo (France)	12 (30)
	John Rutherford (Scotland)	12 (42)

* As at 1 January 2005

— RUGBY GOES DOWN UNDER —

The first game of rugby football played in Australia took place at the Sydney University club in 1864, six years before the game was even introduced to New Zealand.

— BARRY JOHN —

Christened 'the King' by New Zealanders during the 1971 Lions tour, Barry John was a true rugby genius. When he announced his premature retirement from the game in 1972, at the age of only 27, it left the whole of the British Isles – let alone Wales – stunned. He had also starred in Wales's 1971 Grand Slam winning side, and the team that had won the Triple Crown in 1969.

John first played for Wales in 1966 and scored 90 points from his 25 caps. Starting out with Llanelli, he moved to Cardiff and also toured South Africa with the 1968 Lions. Tremendous pace was masked by an economic running style, and the timing and quality of his passing was magnificent. His kicking improved as his career developed, to the extent that by 1971 he was able to torment the All Blacks with the range of his tactical kicking. Allied to that, and his excellent place-kicking, was an almost unnatural ability to score drop goals from any angle, and he scored 180 points on that 1971 Lions tour alone. He also had the easy arrogance and style of the enormously gifted, and from 1970 to 1972 was undoubtedly the biggest star in the world game.

— THE UNION —

In 1870 the game of Rugby football came under attack in the correspondence columns of *The Times* for being dangerous, and as a result there was a growing recognition for the need of an authoritative body. The Rugby Football Union was formed in 1871, and it is surprising that it was a full eight years after the founding of the Football Association that this took place. By the 1860s there were around 20 clubs in London, besides others around the country, playing the Rugby version of football. All of these clubs broadly accepted the laws of Rugby football that had been published by the school, but in the absence of a parent body various clubs still interpreted the rules differently.

— TIMID BAA-BAAS —

The Barbarians – the world-famous invitation-only side – were founded in 1890, but it wasn't until 1957 that they made their first overseas tour, to Canada.

— A WOMAN'S INTUITION? —

The idea of women writing about Lions tours, and women supporters showing their interest in Lions players, is nothing new. Way back in 1955, in a South African newspaper, a female writer by the name of Margaret Lessing revealed that Robin Thompson's Lions found all the attention from females as 'tougher to handle than playing rugby'.

The ladies' favourite among the Lions was 19-year-old flying wing Tony O'Reilly, the baby of the tour but a youngster who made a phenomenal impact on the trip. His famous red hair seemed to send the ladies wild, prompting Lessing to write, 'Britain's touring team have become the pin-up boys of South Africa. Schoolgirl bobby-soxers and women fans are mobbing them wherever they go. Red-headed 19-year-old O'Reilly is pin-up number one, and then comes Johnny Williams, one of 12 players who may settle here, captain Robin Thompson, Jeff Butterfield, Cliff Morgan and Cecil Pedlow.'

— CLIFF MORGAN'S COMMENTARY —

This is how Cliff Morgan described the brilliant length-of-the-field try scored by Gareth Edwards for the Barbarians against New Zealand in 1973:

'The ball is on the halfway line...Kirkpatrick to Williams...[kick ahead]...this is great stuff...Phil Bennett covering...chased by Alistair Scown...brilliant...oh that's brilliant...John Williams [tackled]...Bryan Williams...Pullin...John Dawes...great dummy...David, Tom David...the halfway line...brilliant by Quinnell...this is Gareth Edwards...a dramatic start...what a score!'

— THROTTLING BACK —

In 1863, a set of rules published by the Blackheath Football Club included the line 'Though it is lawful to hold a player in a scrummage, this does not include attempts to throttle or strangle, which are totally opposed to the principles of the game.'

— A BIT OF A COCK-UP —

England's rugby selectors have never really had as poor an image as their cricket counterparts, when it comes to making dumb selections, but in 1906 they certainly made an error of farcical proportions. When Arnold Alcock was chosen to play against South Africa, it soon became apparent that the Guy's Hospital player was out of his depth. The reason? A clerical foul-up had resulted in a selection letter intended for Liverpool's Lancelot Slocock being sent to Alcock instead. Unsurprisingly, Alcock never played for England again, while Slocock – thankfully – went on to represent his country eight times.

— £3 FOR A LIFE BAN —

Welsh student Alban Davies was banned from rugby union *sine die* when, in 1938, he tried to claim £3 for loss of earnings after turning out for Major Stanley's XV. The case, a famous one, underlined British and Irish rugby's determination to remain amateur.

— FIRST-HAND ACCOUNT —

AG Guillemard was one of ten Old Rugbeians to play in England's 20-man team in the first rugby international, against Scotland, at Raeburn Place, Edinburgh, on 27 March 1871. After the match, he wrote an account, which included the following passage: 'The English 20 in this match averaged 12 stone 3 pounds per man, and the Scots probably about the same. JF Green and F Tobin of England and M Cross of Scotland played splendidly behind the scrummage. The Scottish forwards were distinctly quicker on their feet, and in better training than their opponents. Fred Stokes, who learned his football at Rugby, was a most excellent and popular captain of the English 20 for this match and the two succeeding years, combining a thorough knowledge of the game with admirable tact and good temper, and being gifted with the power of infusing spirit and enthusiasm into his team similar to that possessed by AN Hornsby on the cricket field. As a player, he was one of the very best examples of a heavy forward, always on the ball, and first-rate either in the thick of a scrummage or in a loose rally, a good dribbler, very successful in getting the ball when thrown out of touch, a very long drop and a particularly safe tackle. For his club [Blackheath] he often played half back with success as, though not one of the fastest runners, his powers of "shoving off" were very great. He was also one of the very longest and best of place-kicks.'

The 20-man teams that took part in this game were made up of 13 forwards and 7 backs, and the England team had to fund their own hotel and travel expenses. Matches in those days could be won only by a majority of goals – that is, with either a drop goal or a converted try. Tries alone were of no scoring value; they merely allowed a team to *try* for a goal.

Both teams scored unconverted tries, but Scotland's winning goal came when William Cross converted Angus Buchanan's try, early in the second half. This was a controversial effort, after the England scrummage had been pushed back over its own line. The English disputed the legality of the score, but it was awarded by the umpire,* Loretto School's headmaster Dr Almond, who later wrote, 'Let me make a confession. I do not know whether the decision which gave Scotland the try from which the winning goal was kicked was correct, in fact. When an umpire is in doubt, I think he is justified in deciding against the side which makes most noise. They are probably in the wrong.'

---

* Referees did not appear in rugby matches until the mid-1870s.

— THE BAA-BAAS —

The Barbarians Football Club was formed in 1890 by Percy Carpmael, who rejoiced in the nickname of 'Tottie'. Carpmael had been part of a London team who were invited to undertake a tour of the north of England. After one late and convivial dinner in Bradford, he decided that a similar end-of-season jaunt should become a regular feature of the fixture list.

— PRE-TWICKENHAM —

England staged international matches at various venues in the years before Twickenham was built. Here are the venues for the first home meetings with the following:

> v **Scotland** (The Oval, 1872)
> v **Ireland** (The Oval, 1875)
> v **Wales** (Blackheath, 1881)
> v **New Zealand** (Crystal Palace, 1905)
> v **South Africa** (Crystal Palace, 1906)
> v **France** (Richmond, 1907)
> v **Australia** (Blackheath, 1909)

— THE CALCUTTA CUP —

When, in 1877, the Calcutta Rugby Club folded due to a dwindling number of expats working in the Bengal capital, several old boys of Rugby School (who had been at the heart of the club) decided to donate a cup to the Rugby Football Union in memory of their venture. The Calcutta Cup was made from silver rupees and stands 18 inches high. It was formally accepted by the RFU in 1878, and ever since 1879 it has been the trophy awarded to the winners of matches between England and Scotland.

— SCORING A TRY —

The whole of the ball does not need to be in goal for a try to be awarded. Only a part of the ball must touch the in-goal line for the try to stand. Also, a try is awarded if a player puts downward pressure on the grounded ball with another part of his body (between waist and neck) other than his hands.

— TONY O'REILLY —

Ireland's most successful ever international businessman, Sir Anthony O'Reilly, remains the Lions' try-scoring record holder, 45 years after his final Lions tour. AJF O'Reilly, of Old Belvedere and Ireland, scored an astounding 38 tries on just two Lions tours: to South Africa in 1955, with Robin Thompson's side, as an 18-year-old, and to New Zealand in 1959, with Ronnie Dawson's tourists.

O'Reilly, a tall and powerful runner who could break many tackles with his strength and speed, scored only four tries in all the years he played for Ireland (1955–70). But he was never seen at his best in an Irish shirt; instead, it was with the British Lions, in the company of the finest players of the four home unions, that the Irishman really sparkled. His record of six tries in ten Test matches on those 1955 and 1959 tours was exceptional and a record for that time.

O'Reilly made a total of 39 appearances in all his years of international rugby, including ten for the British Isles, giving him a total of 30 points, 18 of which were scored in the Lions' famous red jersey.

Of his two tours, the 1959 visit was the most productive. O'Reilly scored 22 tries in Australia and New Zealand, with 17 of them in New Zealand. Four years earlier, he'd scored 16 tries on the tour. His fellow wing on the 1959 tour, England's Peter Jackson, managed 19 tries, giving them a combined tally of 41 tries on that tour. No wonder those 1959 Lions were known as possessing one of the most exciting back divisions ever assembled. O'Reilly himself, however, believes that the 1955 Lions backs were probably the finest, with the brilliant Welshman Cliff Morgan to launch them from outside-half. As for threatening O'Reilly's record, certainly, no one has come even close to doing so since.

The Irishman's last try for the 1955 Lions came in the fourth Test, when he was late-tackled after crossing the line and touching down for a try. The impact broke his collarbone, an injury about which O'Reilly says ruefully 48 years later, 'It was an injury of which I am reminded every morning when I get up.'

— HONEYMOON BLISS —

WJA 'Dave' Davies was one of England's outstanding fly-halves and captains, despite being Welsh-born. In 1923, his retirement season, he even arranged for his honeymoon to be spent in Paris so that he could lead England to the fourth Grand Slam of his career with a victory over France at the Stade Colombes.

— FLOODLIT RUGBY —

The first instances of rugby matches being played under floodlights came in the 1878/9 season. With electricity companies seeking to promote the new method of lighting – in direct competition with the gas companies – a craze for illuminated sporting events quickly spread around the country. The first recorded floodlit rugby match took place on 22 October 1878, when two powerful lights suspended from 30-foot-high poles provided illumination enough for the meeting of Broughton and Swinton. Another floodlit match in the Liverpool area was staged later in the same month, and subsequent illuminated games went ahead at Hawick, Kelso and Newport.

— THEY THINK IT'S ALL OVER...IT IS NOW —

Commentator Kenneth Wolstenholme's immortal line, in reaction to Geoff Hurst's decisive hat-trick (and England's fourth) goal in the 1966 football World Cup final against West Germany at Wembley, was at last challenged when Jonny Wilkinson kicked the goal that won England a rugby World Cup. BBC Radio's rugby correspondent Ian Robertson captured the moment brilliantly with the following words on Radio 5 Live: 'There's 35 seconds to go. This is the one. It's coming back to Jonny Wilkinson. He drops for World Cup glory. It's up! It's over! He's done it! Jonny Wilkinson is England's hero – yet again. And there's no time for Australia to come back. England have just won the World Cup.'

As ex-Scottish international fly-half Robertson spoke, listeners could hear his supposedly impartial summariser, former England fly-half and Wilkinson's mentor Rob Andrew, shrieking hysterically with joy in the background. 'I elbowed him in the ribs, and he cracked his head on the chair in front,' said Robertson later. 'It served him right. He was totally unprofessional!'

— IN MEMORIAM 2 —

The Second World War claimed the lives of 111 international rugby players from around the world. Among them was the celebrated White Russian prince, Alexander Obolensky, who was born in Leningrad but went on to represent England and, in 1936, score one of the most famous tries in rugby history. Obolensky, in fact, scored twice in England's victory over the All Blacks at Twickenham, but it is his second score – courtesy of a scything run – that has gained immortality. Prince Obolensky joined the RAF when war was declared, and was killed when his Hawker Hurricane plane crashed on landing in East Anglia.

— THE 57 OLD FARTS —

England captain Will Carling gave an unwitting voice to those crying out for change in rugby union when, in an off-microphone moment following a 1995 television interview, he referred to those running English rugby as '57 old farts'.

Carling was being interviewed by Greg Dyke for a Yorkshire Television documentary and, after a recorded interview, he unpinned his voice microphone and placed it on the table in front of him. Continuing to chat, Dyke asked Carling about the game being run by committee and the England skipper replied, 'If the game is run properly as a professional game, you do not need 57 old farts running rugby.' *The Sun* newspaper subsequently got wind of what Carling had said – and the microphone had picked up – and published it. The RFU were distinctly unamused, and said that they would sack Carling from his post. However, Rob Andrew and Dean Richards – the two England players most likely to be offered the post should Carling be stood down – both issued statements to the effect that they did not intend to take over the job in such circumstances, and in the end the RFU backed down and Carling led England to the 1995 World Cup.

— HOW IT BEGAN: ITALY —

Rugby was introduced to Italy by students and workers returning from France in the early 1900s. The game expanded so rapidly in certain areas of the country that, by 1929, Italy was able to play its first international, against Spain, which they lost 9–0.

— POINTS SCORING —

The awarding of points for scores did not occur in international rugby until 1886, and even then there was no uniformity of scoring values until England joined the International Board, in 1891.

— CAMPO'S POEM —

Australian wing David Campese was the undoubted star of the 1991 World Cup, even getting away with what seemed to be a deliberate try-saving knock-forward (rather than an attempted interception) to prevent Peter Winterbottom from setting free an overlapping Rory Underwood for a try that would have put England 12–9 up in the second half of the Twickenham final. Wherever the charismatic Campese went, he carried with him the following poem by Nancye Sims, which was given to him by his mother and which he made sure he read before every game he played:

> Winners take chances.
> Like everyone else, they fear failing but refuse to let fear control them.
> Winners don't give up.
> When life gets rough, they hang in until the going gets better.
> Winners are flexible.
> They realise there is more than one way and are willing to try others.
> Winners know they are not perfect.
> They respect their weaknesses while making the most of their strengths.
> Winners fall, but they don't stay down.
> They stubbornly refuse to let a fall keep them from climbing...
> Winners don't blame fate for their failures nor luck for their success.
> Winners accept responsibility for their lives.
> Winners are positive thinkers who see good in all things.
> From the ordinary, they make the extraordinary.
> Winners believe in the path they have chosen even when it's hard,
> Even when others can't see where they are going.
> Winners are patient.
> They know a goal is only as worthy as the effort required to achieve it.
> Winners are people like you.
> They make this place a better place to be.

— FOUL PLAY BY DOG —

Oxford University forward George Podmore was bitten by a stray dog that had wandered onto the Parker's Piece ground in Cambridge during the 1873 Varsity match. To add insult to injury for poor Podmore, Cambridge University emerged as winners by a goal and two tries to nil.

— 15-ALL —

Until 1877, when England played Ireland at the Oval, London, all international matches had been 20-a-side affairs. Teams normally lined up with 13 forwards, three half backs, one three-quarter back and three full backs. Mauls consisted of 26 forwards battling to propel the ball, or ball-carrier, forward, and backs got their hands on the ball only occasionally. Passing movements between the backs were virtually non-existent.

Anyone running with the ball usually found themselves confronted by a wall of opponents, and the laws in place at the time decreed that a tackled player had to call 'down' when he was held. At that, both sets of forwards gathered around the tackled player, who then placed the ball on the ground. A scrum was then formed around the ball, and both packs proceeded to try to shove the other backwards. Often the ball was propelled downfield by a mass dribble. Scrums and mauls were largely long-drawn-out affairs, during which no heeling was allowed, or wheeling.

The subsequent lack of entertainment value in these early rugby matches – with the ball often caught up in a mêlée and rendered invisible – soon caused the authorities to address this problem by tinkering with the laws and reducing teams to 15 per side. Oxford and Cambridge Universities had pioneered the 15-a-side game in 1875, and thus the England v Ireland game 18 months later became the first international played under 'modern' rules. In this match, too, spectators were also treated to the then unique sight of Lancashire Test cricketer Albert Hornsby employing the tactic of punting downfield to win ground. It was Hornsby's first appearance as an England rugby player, at the age of almost 30.

— GET ME TO THE MATCH ON TIME —

John Macauley, a big and bustling forward from Limerick, was so desperate to play in Ireland's February 1887 international against England in Dublin that he got married. The reason? Macauley, a miller's agent, had by then used up all his holiday entitlement and his employers wouldn't allow him any more time off. He obtained the necessary leave of absence by claiming the automatic holiday afforded to a newlywed. According to contemporary reports, his new wife 'fully endorsed the enthusiasm'.

Moreover, Macauley's heroic commitment to the Irish cause was not without further reward. After 11 defeats and a draw in their previous 12 meetings, Ireland finally won an historic triumph over England by two converted tries to nil.

— DOUBLE TAKE —

The only man to have represented two home unions in the International Championship was James Marsh, who first represented Scotland in 1889 and then England in 1892. What's more, Marsh only ever won three international caps in total, his first two while in the dark-blue jersey of Scotland (gained while a medical student at Edinburgh University) and his sole England appearance against Ireland at Manchester in 1892, after he had settled in the area as a GP. The Irish were most confused: his powerful tackling and kicking from hand had helped the Scots to beat them in Belfast three years earlier.

— KEN JONES —

Wales wing Ken Jones won a silver medal at the 1948 London Olympics, running in the British 4 x 100m relay team.

— GRAND NATIONAL WINNERS —

The game of rugby can boast two men who also know what it's like to win at the highest level in racing. In 1928, a 100–1 outsider named Tipperary Tim ran to Grand National victory at Aintree, 29 years after his owner, Irishman John Ryan, had helped his country to Triple Crown rugby success. Then, in 1979, former Scotland number eight John Douglas – who gained a dozen caps in the early 1960s – saw his horse Rubstic also come in first in the National.

— THE MONOCLED INTERNATIONAL —

The splendidly named Ireland full back Dolway Walkington was so short-sighted that he once took to the field for an international against Wales at Llanelli's Stradey Park while wearing a monocle. Despite his myopia, however, late on in this 1891 championship game he fielded a loose Welsh kick out of defence, removed his monocle, steadied himself and calmly dropped a goal.

— FOOTBALL 1, RUGBY 0 —

In April 1892, a unique four-part sporting challenge saw a team of footballers under the Corinthians banner defeat a Barbarians XV that included several members of England's International Championship-winning pack...at rugby. The Corinthians – who had the world-class all-round sportsman CB Fry among their number – won 14-12, with Tom Lindley scoring two tries. Two days earlier, Lindley had scored a hat-trick as the soccer players defeated the rugby players 6–0 in a round-ball contest. The four-sport challenge, which also included athletics and cricket, was won 3-1 by the Corinthians, who had initiated the event as part of a charity festival.

— THE CASINO KING —

Francis Haget, who played for France from 1974 to 1987, used to work as a croupier at the casino in Biarritz.

— RADIO FIRST —

The first live radio commentary of a British sporting event took place at Twickenham in January 1927, when the BBC employed Captain Teddy Wakelam – a former player with Harlequins – to describe the England–Wales rugby international. In *The Times*, the perceptive Bernard Darwin wrote, 'In the course of time, all sports and leading outdoor events will be so reported.'

HAVE YOU HEARD THE ONE ABOUT THE SCOTSMAN, — THE SCOTSMAN AND THE SCOTSMAN? —

Uniquely, in the first Test match of the 1903 British/Irish tour of South Africa, the two captains for the game and the referee were all Scottish internationals. The tourists were led by Mark Morrison, a farmer who had just led Scotland to the Triple Crown, and the South Africans were skippered by Alex Frew, who two years earlier had played under Morrison in another Triple Crown-winning Scottish side and soon afterwards emigrated to South Africa to practise medicine in the Transvaal. Bill Donaldson, the referee, had played six times for Scotland in the 1890s.

— A FULL HOUSE —

The first international player to achieve rugby's 'full house' of scores – try, conversion, penalty and dropped goal – was Wales's Jerry Shea, in a 19–5 victory against England at Swansea in January 1920.

— LOST IN THE FOG —

Those who were there swear it's true, but it's still a story that might have been embellished with the telling. In Bristol in 1908 a dense fog descended on the International Championship match between England and Wales. The Welsh won 28–18, but conditions were verging on the farcical and one player recorded afterwards that in the second half neither spectators nor stands could be seen from the middle of the field. Indeed, after the match the Wales team were relaxing in hot tubs in their dressing room when it was realised that full back Bert Winfield was missing. A team official went back outside on to the pitch, called his name, and was astonished when Winfield appeared out of the fog. The Cardiff man had apparently thought that his team were merely keeping up an attacking position, and that he was required to maintain a defensive watch.

— POINTS EVOLUTION —

England were the first country to try to introduce a points system to determine the outcome of matches when, in 1886, they designated a try as being worth one point and a goal (which was a converted try) as three points. Until then, all matches had been declared draws unless a goal had been scored. Initially, all the other home unions refused to accept this system, and it wasn't in general use until in 1892, when the value of the try was upgraded to two points.

	TRY	CONVERSION	PENALTY	DROP
1891	1	2	2	3
1892–3	2	3	3	4
1894–5	3	2	3	4
1896–1947	3	2	3	3
1948–71	3	2	3	3
1972–91	4	2	3	3
1992–present	5	2	3	3

— OFF THE BENCH —

Replacements were not allowed at all until 1968, and then only in internationals and certain other representative games. For instance, in the 1973 National Knockout Competition (which in 1975 came to be known as the John Player Cup), Bristol were condemned to play virtually the entire match with 14 men after John Pullin, their England hooker, hobbled off with a serious knee injury just minutes into the contest. They eventually lost 27–15 to Coventry.

Meanwhile, on the Lions tour of South Africa in 1968, Ireland's Barry Bresnihan became the game's first-ever replacement, coming on for his compatriot Mike Gibson in the opening fixture against Western Transvaal at Potchefstroom.

— GETTING SHIRTY —

Scottish prop-forward Jock Wemyss was ready to take to the field bare-chested in Paris on New Year's Day, 1920, in protest at the tight-fisted attitude of the Scotland selectors.

Unlike the rest of the Scottish team, Wemyss had not been handed a shirt in the dressing room before that match against France, on the basis that he had also been selected to play international rugby before the First World War. The forthcoming match was the first Scotland were to play since the Great War had ended – and the Scottish officials demanded to know what Wemyss had done with the shirt he had worn six years earlier. They argued that he should still have had it, and didn't believe him, either, when he protested that he had actually swapped it with an opponent. As a result, Wemyss stood in the tunnel in just his shorts, socks and boots (his own, of course) until, at the last minute before the teams walked out, the Scottish official in charge gave in to this act of brinksmanship and threw him another shirt.

A fascinating postscript to this tale is that, during the match, Wemyss – who had lost an eye in the War – packed down against Marcel Lubin-Lebrere, who had also lost an eye in the conflict. Afterwards, at the post-match dinner, the two struck up a tremendous friendship that was to last well beyond the end of their respective playing careers.

— FRESH BLOOD —

The Wales team that began the 1934 international season showed quite a number of changes from the one that had ended the 1933 championship – 15, to be precise. Talk about bringing in new blood. Wales then lost the opening match of 1934 – against England at Cardiff – by 9–0, after which the selectors were roundly, and unsurprisingly, criticised.

— DALLAGLIO'S RECORD —

Lawrence Dallaglio, who preceded and succeeded Martin Johnson as England's rugby captain, was the only England player to be on the pitch for every minute of the successful 2003 World Cup campaign.

— WARTIME TESTS —

Only two senior international matches have taken place during wartime: in August 1914, just after the outbreak of the First World War, Australia played New Zealand in Sydney; and in February 1940 a British Army XV full of seasoned internationals played France in Paris in a match for which the French awarded caps. This last fixture, played some five months after the start of the Second World War, thus stands as the only official international ever staged on a continent at war.

— EARLY FOOTBALL WRITINGS —

Besides 12th-century chronicler Fitzstephen, there are accounts of early football games from other sources which tell clearly of the popularity (and violence) of the precursors of rugby. In his 1602 *Survey Of Cornwall*, Richard Carew writes of the game hurling: 'The play is verily both rough and rude… When the hurling is ended you shall see them returning home as from a pitched battle with bloody pates, bones broken and out of joint, and such bruises as serve to shorten their days.' By this time, Cornish hurling had developed many rugby-like features, including an offside rule and a limiting of the participants to 15, 20 or 30 players per side.

Writing about cnapan in 1603, when it was already centuries old, historian George Owen of Pembrokeshire asserts that it was a handling game played with a small, round wooden ball that was carried cross-country by two opposing teams that could number, in total, 2,000 people. Injuries were many, and sometimes there were even fatalities. Owen could have been penning words for the idealistic amateur Victorians of almost three centuries later when he wrote, 'The players contend not for any wager or valuable thing, but for glory and renown – first for the game and their country in general, next every particular to win praise for his activity and prowess…which two considerations ardently inflameth the minds of youthful people to strive to the death for glory and fame.'

— NIL–NIL —

The last three 0–0 scorelines in international rugby all occurred in the early 1960s: England v Wales at Twickenham in 1962, Ireland v England in Dublin in 1963, and Scotland v New Zealand at Murrayfield in 1964. The Swinging Sixties were not exactly being mirrored on the rugby field, were they?

— ENGLAND'S CHANGE OF TACTICS —

Many commentators on the game have theorised since the 1991 World Cup final about whether England lost the game by changing from a 10-man to a free-flowing 15-man tactical approach, or whether Australia won it by matching the English forwards for muscle and sinew and grafting on to this effort a heroic and well-drilled defence. Paul Ackford, the England lock and now rugby correspondent of the *Sunday Telegraph*, recalls, 'When it came to the final, we could not transfer the excellence of the unopposed training sessions we had in the build-up to the game to the intensity of the live match itself. Around half-time, when we started to get on top of the big Aussie forwards, we should have thrown the running rugby option out of the window. We didn't, and the rest is history.'

Following England's 12–6 defeat, their coach, Geoff Cooke, said, 'We decided to change our tactics as a team. The players agreed. Australia went into that game with three players with experience of playing in the full-back position: Roebuck, Egerton and Campese. If we'd kicked to them, they all could have positioned themselves to respond, and to do so to our disadvantage. They also had a very powerful pack. They expected us to play in our usual style and they had already beaten us 40–15 in Sydney, three months or so earlier.

'Rugby is a game of tactics, to out-think the opposition. In the pre-match build-up, the players were comfortable with the change.'

— TWO IN ONE —

New Zealand holds the unique distinction of being the only country ever to have fielded two different teams on the same day for fully fledged cap internationals. It happened on Saturday, 3 September 1949, although the All Blacks might have regretted their decision after both matches were lost. A virtual third-string XV took on Australia in Wellington, where the Wallabies won 11–6, and later on the same day the first-choice All Blacks lost 9–3 to South Africa in Durban.

— THE VIVIAN JENKINS TRY —

In these modern times, it's a barely believable fact that, prior to 1962, only one full back had scored a try in the International Championship. However, until the 1968/9 law which ruled that direct-kicking into touch outside the 25-yard (or 22m) line was banned, the role of the rugby full back was almost always the rigid defensive one of providing a last line of defence and kicking the ball into touch to set up field position.

In March 1934, though, a centre three-quarter by the name of Vivian Jenkins defied the accepted customs of his day by first initiating a late Wales attack by running from within his own 25, and then following up the ensuing movement to be on hand to gather up a loose ball and canter over the Ireland line for the first score of the match. It proved to be the catalyst of a great Welsh surge that included two more tries in the last five minutes, resulting in a 13–0 win. After the final whistle, however, Bridgend's Jenkins was castigated by rugby purists for not kicking into touch in defence when he first received the ball.

— WILLIAM WEBB ELLIS —

The canonisation of former Rugby School pupil William Webb Ellis as the inventor of rugby football came after his death in 1872, and owes much to the administrators of the new sport needing a romantic myth to account for the birth of the game. Many of the first administrators were Old Rugbeians, too, so it served them well that the school should thus be linked forever with the creation of a 'new' and popular game.

Webb Ellis was by most accounts an unpopular boy and – by common consent – got away with running with the ball in the historic school match only because he was by then a senior pupil. He left Rugby School in 1825, to go to Brasenose College in Oxford. He then took holy orders before joining St Clement's Dane Church in the Strand, London. He died in France on 24 January 1872, and was thought never to have picked up a rugby ball again after the day he left school.

It is ironic that the 'founder' of the game contributed so little to its subsequent growth, but that many other former pupils of Rugby School had so much to do with that growth and the game's future administration. William Webb Ellis, however, has long since served his purpose.

— THE COHENS —

Northampton wing Ben Cohen made it a unique family double when he played in England's World Cup-winning rugby team in 2003. His uncle, George Cohen, who was in Sydney to watch his nephew's triumph, had been a member of England's 1966 World Cup-winning soccer team.

— TOP 10 MOST INTERNATIONAL CONVERSIONS* —

1   Andrew Mehrtens (New Zealand) ....169 (70 matches)
2   Michael Lynagh (Australia) 140 (72)
3   Neil Jenkins (Wales) 130 (87)
4   Diego Dominguez (Italy) 127 (74)
5   Jonny Wilkinson (England) 123 (52)
6   Grant Fox (New Zealand) 118 (46)
7   Matthew Burke (Australia) 104 (81)
8   Nicky Little (Fiji) 99 (53)
9   Gavin Hastings (Scotland) 86 (61)
10   Ronan O'Gara (Ireland) 80 (47)

* As at 1 January 2005

— THE NAME GAME —

In September 1950, two men named George Nepia faced each other in a first-class fixture between Poverty Bay and the Olympians invitation club in Gisborne, New Zealand. They were father and son, and both played full back. The senior man, a veteran of the All Blacks' unbeaten 1924/5 tour of Britain and France and by then 45 years old, became the oldest New Zealander to feature in a first-class match. And he finished on the winning side.

— REPLACEMENTS —

Replacements for injured players were often allowed in New Zealand v Australia internationals during the 60 or more years that preceded the International Rugby Board's official sanctioning of their use in 1968. It was therefore fitting, given the two countries' far-sightedness, that All Black forward Ian Kirkpatrick became the first replacement to score a Test hat-trick of tries in the very first New Zealand v Australia international that took place in 1968 under the new IRB sanctions. Kirkpatrick had come on in the 25th minute to replace the injured Brian Lochore.

— LONG-RUNNING JOHNNO —

Martin Johnson, England's World Cup-winning captain, has played more games of professional rugby than anyone else. He had already played many matches before the sport actually turned professional in August 1995 – including his first 16 caps for England – but the giant lock's pro tally was up around the 350 mark at the midway point of the 2004–5 season.

— THE SECRET OF '71 —

Many people believed that the secret behind the success of the 1971 British Lions in New Zealand was the combination of their manager – big, burly Scotsman Dr Doug Smith – and their quiet but brilliantly gifted coach, Welshman Carwyn James.

James had never coached his national side, and his selection caused uproar in some quarters. His critics felt that the Lions coach should always come from the four home unions' coaches list, but James broke the trend.

Smith proved himself a popular manager, but also a brilliant prophet. Before the tour even started, he forecast that the Lions would win the four-match Test series 2–1, with one match drawn. That was precisely what happened.

The Lions side won a 9–3 victory at the first Test, in Dunedin (a game in which the gutsy Scottish prop Ian McLauchlan – known to one and all as 'Mighty Mouse' – scored a crucial try), lost the second Test 22–12, again in Dunedin, but won the third 13–3 in Wellington. That made it 2–1 in the series, and just as Smith had prophesied, the fourth Test was drawn, 14–14, thanks in no small part to a rare act: a soaring drop goal by Lions full back JPR Williams. It put the Lions into the history books because, at that time, not even the greatest of all the touring Springbok sides in history had ever managed to win a Test series in New Zealand.

James masterminded the triumph with his quiet, calm, intuitive scheming. He believed in allowing the backs freedom to play and told his forwards, 'If you just win us 30–40 per cent of possession, I believe we have the backs to take the series.' The forwards achieved that against a powerful New Zealand pack containing the great Colin Meads, and James was right – when it came to moving the ball down the two back lines, the genius of the Lions players put them in a class of their own.

Only one other side toppled the great 1971 Lions: Queensland, in the first match of the tour, during a brief two-match stopover in Australia before arriving in New Zealand.

The last laugh, however, was had by the Lions, because after the Australian province had beaten the Lions 15–11, some New Zealand critics who had travelled across the Tasman Sea for the game wrote, 'It isn't worth these Lions even turning up in New Zealand, because they'll get such a thrashing.'

— WORLD CUP VENUES: SOUTH AFRICA —

— STICK IT UP YOUR JUMPER —

This is a well-worn rugby phrase used to signal an intent to keep the ball tight. In an Australian inter-provincial match in May 1975, however, the ball was literally stuck up underneath a player's jersey in a bizarre but highly effective tap penalty routine that led directly to a match-winning try being scored.

A group of players lined up in a shallow crescent with their backs to the opposing line and, as the ball was being passed down the line like a pass-the-parcel game, each player (including the one actually with the ball) made it look as if they had shoved the ball up their jerseys and turned to run in all directions. The player with the ball, Greg Cornelson, ran 15m before taking the ball out from under his top. It was too late for the defending side to cover the danger and, two passes later, a try had been scored. When more sides tried to mimic this move in the following weeks, the Australian authorities referred the up-the-jumper tactic to the International Rugby Board, who ruled it illegal.

— PULLIN'S PUNCH-LINE —

In 1972, at the height of the Irish troubles, both Scotland and Wales decided against travelling to Dublin for their Five Nations Championship matches. The following year, however, despite continuing problems in Ulster and tension in the Republic, John Pullin's England team decided to travel and fulfil their fixture. Pullin's team received a rapturous Lansdowne Road welcome and, after his side had been beaten 18–9, the English captain also brought the house down when he quipped, 'Well, we might not be much good, but at least we turn up!'

— WHEN MANDELA WAS JUST A — FACE IN THE CROWD

It is estimated that the first Test match between South Africa and the touring British Lions in 1955 was watched by the biggest ever rugby crowd in the world at that time. Johannesburg's Ellis Park ground was packed for the match, and it's believed that up to 105,000 people may have crammed in for the game. One of them, standing quietly in the fenced-off section for black supporters, was a certain Nelson Mandela.

However many were there, they witnessed a crackerjack of a match, with the Lions just hanging on for a 23–22 win, the most number of points ever totalled for a Test match in South Africa at that time.

The Lions won when South African full back Jack van der Schyff missed the conversion of a last-minute try that would have given his team victory. The missed kick was costly for the Springboks and van der Schyff: the side lost the Test and he was promptly dropped, never to play for South Africa again.

A famous photograph was taken of the moment when van der Schyff knew that his kick had just failed, his head slumped onto his shoulders as the ball veered away to the left. The photograph was wired around the world, a vivid reminder of what it meant to rugby-mad South Africans to lose any Test match.

— THE LIONS ARE NAMED —

The 1924 British Isles team, captained by Dr Ronald Cove-Smith of Old Merchant Taylors and England, played 21 matches on its tour of South Africa but won only nine. However, it was the first team to be known as the 'British Lions', a nickname gained due to the logos on their tour ties.

Previous touring sides had been known as the 'British Isles Rugby Union Team', but the 'Lions' was seen as a more concise title. The name stuck and every subsequent touring team from Britain has been known by one and all as the Lions.

— COLD DAY, HEATED DEBATE —

The winter of 1962–3 was so cold that the January Five Nations Championship clash between Wales and England at Cardiff featured national anthems that were played with both sets of players remaining in their dressing rooms in order to keep warm.

In fact, it was a miracle that the match was played at all, as 30 tons of straw were laid on the pitch during the week to protect the surface from snow and a biting wind. Terraces were salted copiously and snow cleared so that spectators could safely attend. The previous five weeks had seen club rugby and football programmes virtually wiped out by the weather, and both the Wales and England teams were issued with thermal underwear. Several Welsh backs wore gloves.

The match attracted a massive television audience, not just because of the inherent grudge-match interest but also because the sporting public had been so starved of any live action. England won the game 13–6, their last win in Cardiff for 28 years, but heated debates followed about whether the match should have gone ahead at all. Players had been slipping and sliding around on the frozen surface right from the kick-off, after the game had begun in temperatures of minus six. No one was seriously injured, but most players finished up nursing cuts, grazes and friction burns.

— KILLED BY LIGHTNING —

Jean-François Philiponeau, one of France's most talented international wings of the era, was killed in May 1976 by a bolt of lightning while he played in a friendly match for his club, Montferrand. He was 25.

— SAVED BY AN OPPONENT —

Rugby is, of course, a hard and tough sport where knocking seven bells out of an opponent is part and parcel of the deal. However, on one occasion, in November 1966, it was actually an opponent who came to the aid of Newport centre Gordon Britton, and probably even saved his life.

The incident occurred late on during a fiercely contested game between the Rodney Parade club and the visiting Australian touring team. Britton was hit by a double tackle from two Wallabies that was perfectly legal, but an accidental clash of heads left him writhing on the ground. Players from both sides soon realised that Britton was convulsing and in great distress. Luckily, and before Newport's medical adviser Dr John Miles could rush out on to the field, Wallaby number eight John O'Gorman – a qualified doctor – came to Britton's aid and saw that the Newport player had half-swallowed his tongue. He was struggling to breathe and had rapidly turned first grey and then blue. O'Gorman reached into Britton's mouth and brought his tongue back into its proper position, and soon Dr Miles was also on hand to administer mouth-to-mouth resuscitation. Happily, Britton immediately began to breathe more easily and, in the end, suffered no more than concussion.

— FIJIANS: THE WORLD'S BEST? —

There were no World Cups in those days, but the 1970 Fijians could still claim to be one of the best rugby sides on the planet after their remarkable 29–9 dismantling of a star-studded Barbarians side at Gosforth in Newcastle. With forwards running and handling like backs, and with all their players showing power and pace in every area of the field, the Fijian side ran in seven tries against one of the best British teams ever assembled. Indeed, more than half of the Barbarian team humbled on that October afternoon became leading members of the 1971 British Lions side that won an historic series victory in New Zealand.

— MODELS V ACTRESSES —

In September 1974, a charity match was staged at London Irish's ground at Sunbury-on-Thames between a team of models and a team of actresses. Unsurprisingly, given the short length of most of the shorts and the tightness of most of the shirts, a large crowd turned up to witness a 10–10 draw.

— THE MOST FAMOUS STREAK OF ALL? —

Like many crazes, it started in America, but in Britain at least no streaker has ever had as big an impact on public perception as rugby's Erika Roe. Few now remember that it was Michael O'Brien's streak at Twickenham during the 1974 England v Wales international that started the craze for stripping off at big sporting occasions on this side of the pond, but everyone recalls Miss Roe.

The 24 year old from Hampshire certainly had at least a couple of things going for her, as was amply demonstrated when she took it upon herself to remove her top and cavort on the field during the half-time interval of England's tense January 1982 international against Australia. The incident made headlines in all the newspapers (with pictures, of course), but perhaps the best comment of all was made by one of the England players during the streak.

England's captain, Bill Beaumont, had been in the middle of an impassioned half-time team talk on one side of the pitch (no one spent the interval in the dressing rooms in those days) when Erika bounced into view behind him. Suddenly, Big Bill was aware that his players were no longer paying attention to what he was saying. When he asked what the matter was, one replied, 'It's because there's a girl running around over there with your bum on her chest.' Beaumont's braves were suitably inspired, either by his words or by the sight of Miss Roe: despite having to play into the wind in the second half, they converted their interval 6–3 lead into a 15–11 victory.

— GRAND SLAM WINNERS —

ENGLAND (12)	1913, 1914, 1921, 1923, 1924, 1928, 1957, 1980, 1991, 1992, 1995, 2003
WALES (8)	1908, 1909, 1911, 1950, 1952, 1971, 1976, 1978
FRANCE (8)	1968, 1977, 1981, 1987, 1997, 1998, 2002, 2004
SCOTLAND (3)	1925, 1984, 1990
IRELAND (1)	1948

— SOME OBSCURE RUGBY UNION RULES —

- If a drop-out crosses the 10m line (ie its minimum required journey) but is then blown back by a strong wind, play shall continue.

- If a conversion kick, penalty or drop goal goes over the bar, but is then blown back by a strong wind, the goal will count.

- A mark made 'in goal' can result in a scrummage 5m from the in-goal line if the player opts for it.

- A player can kick or propel the ball with his hand if he is partly in touch. However, he cannot catch the ball while part of him is in touch.

- If a player is lying on the ground, injured, and is hit by the ball, or ball carrier, when in an offside position, he is deemed to be 'accidentally offside' and is not penalised. Play continues, unless that player's team gets an unfair advantage, in which case a scrum would be ordered.

- A penalty is awarded against any player who deliberately throws a ball into touch, touch in goal or over the dead-ball line.

— RUGBY FIELD POSITIONS —

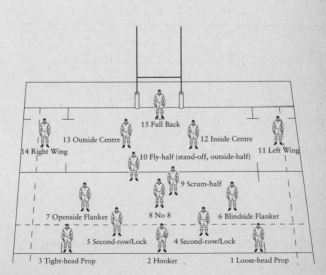

15 Full Back
13 Outside Centre
12 Inside Centre
14 Right Wing
11 Left Wing
10 Fly-half (stand-off, outside-half)
9 Scrum-half
7 Openside Flanker
8 No 8
6 Blindside Flanker
5 Second-row/Lock
4 Second-row/Lock
3 Tight-head Prop
2 Hooker
1 Loose-head Prop

— VIDEO REF —

The first international use of the video referee occurred during the New Zealand v Tonga match at Albury, near Auckland, in June 2000. Steve Lander, the English referee, consulted with Kiwi official Steve Walsh in the stands before awarding a try to All Black captain Todd Blackadder following a mass maul that had crashed over the Tongan line.

— BATH v WIGAN —

In May 1996, Bath – then the undisputed kings of English rugby union – met Wigan, who held that position in rugby league, in a special two-match cross-code challenge to celebrate the end of 100 years of hostility between the two sports. The result was a decisive moral victory for the league boys, who displayed a superiority in lines of running, consistency of tackling and basic skills that left the union players gasping.

The first leg of the challenge was a league match played at Maine Road, Manchester, which Wigan won 82–6, running in 16 tries, with former union wing Martin Offiah crossing six times. In the second leg, played under union rules at Twickenham, Wigan also distinguished themselves with three thrilling tries and some gutsy defence, although Bath ran out 44–19 winners.

— HALPIN'S VOLVO —

London Irish captain and prop Garry Halpin held up a Pilkington Cup semi-final tie against Leicester at Sunbury in March 1996 so that he could fetch his keys from the dressing room and get a friend in the crowd to move his car. Just as he was about to pack down for a scrummage, Halpin had heard the PA announcer give out the registration number of his Volvo and warn that the police intended to remove it from the ground unless it was immediately moved to a more appropriate place. Irish, only 22—21 down at that point in the match, went on to lose 46–21. But at least Halpin didn't lose his car to a clamping compound.

— HOW IT BEGAN: NEW ZEALAND —

The man responsible for taking the game to New Zealand, where it has since become the undisputed national sport, was Charles Monro. On his return home to the country in 1870, having played the game at school in England, he introduced the Rugby School rules of football to locals in his home town of Nelson, on the South Island, and found his countrymen to be immediately receptive to the game, incorporating as it does both strength and skill.

The other reason for rugby's rapid growth in New Zealand was the way that it was quickly embraced by the native Maori people, as much as by the European immigrant population.

— AS EASY AS ABC —

In the days before professional rugby led to more dull conformity, many rugby teams wore letters of the alphabet on the backs of their jerseys for identification, instead of numbers. International sides have had standardised numbering since 1967, when the IRB ruled that it should be so, but club sides could have lettering or odd numbering right up to the birth of the professional era, in 1995.

Bristol and Leicester are the two most famous British examples of clubs who traditionally used letters on shirts, although Bristol labelled their players from A to O, starting from the full back, while Leicester began with the front row and worked backwards from there. Hence, in the period directly before the birth of professionalism, the celebrated Tigers front-row trio of Darren Garforth, Richard Cockerill and Graham Rowntree was widely known as the 'ABC Club'. And when Leicester met Bristol in the 1983 John Player Cup final at Twickenham, the jumble of letters on display – with players in similar positions having different letters on their backs – prompted at least one observer to remark that it looked more like a game of rugby scrabble.

— WHAT'S IN A NAME? —

In the British Isles, a fly-half is also often called a stand-off, outside-half or out-half. In the southern hemisphere, the man wearing the number ten shirt is commonly referred to as the first five-eighth. Whatever he is called, he is one of the most important players on the field, shaping the whole tactical approach of his team.

— GLADIATORS THRUST INTO BIG ARENA —

They might have been Dorset's finest – in the bar, that is – but the motley collection of rugby veterans who toured Romania as the Dorchester Gladiators over Easter 2000 got the shock of their lives when they turned up for one of their fixtures.

It had come about through the influence of an official at the Bucharest Embassy who had met them when they were distributing toys to an orphanage and asked if they would like him to fix up a match. Clearly, he thought they were more than just an amateur outfit, because when the men from Dorchester arrived at the venue they discovered that it was the National Stadium, their opponents were crack club side Steaua Bucharest, there were several thousand spectators already in the ground…and the match was being televised live on Romanian TV!

Despite the Dorset team's protests about their abilities, the Romanians realised the awful truth only once the game had begun. After falling quickly behind as the hosts piled up early points, the Gladiators were extremely glad that the Romanian players eased off in the second half. At the final whistle, which confirmed a 60–17 defeat, the stout men of Dorset were actually quite pleased with their one-off performance on the big stage. And of course, once they'd repaired to the after-match bar, the Dorchester Gladiators proved that they were more than a match for their opponents.

— GUSCOTT'S TREK —

Former Bath, England and British Lions centre Jeremy Guscott walked more than 800 miles (the equivalent of a marathon a day for a month) and visited all of the Zurich Premiership rugby clubs during his 'Tetley's Trek' – a charity walk on behalf of leukaemia research – in the autumn of 2001. He finished his long march by striding into Twickenham and out onto the pitch during half-time at an England v Australia international.

— SCOT OR NOT? —

Former Bristol butcher Dave Hilton made 41 appearances for Scotland in the 1990s before it was discovered that he was not, in fact, eligible for them, after wrongly believing that one of his grandparents had been born north of the border. After the IRB tightened up their qualification rules, Hilton requalified for Scotland by residence and, three years later, won his 42nd cap when he came on as a replacement during the November 2002 victory against South Africa.

— MAX BOYCE —

Welsh rugby wouldn't be quite the same without entertainer Max Boyce, who has acted as an unofficial bard of the Welsh national game for more than three decades. He first came to prominence – boasting his famous catchphrase 'I was there!' – during the glory days of Wales rugby in the 1970s, with his popular TV show *Poems And Pints*, on which he sang songs and told tales about the Welsh fly-half factory and the deeds of Gareth, Barry, Gerald, JJ and JPR.

One such example was his joke about the time that Wales were playing England at Twickenham and the crowds were such that many travelling Welshmen were locked out. One little Welsh supporter went around to the back of one of the big stands and, seeing a tall Englishman looking down at him from on high, shouted up to him to tell him what was happening. A big roar had just gone up, and the Welshman wanted to know what it was for. 'Well, there's been a big punch-up and the whole of the Welsh team, bar Gareth Edwards, have been sent off the field by the referee,' boomed down the Englishman. Several minutes later there was another huge roar from the crowd and the little Welshman called up, 'What's happenin'? What's happenin'? Gareth scored, 'ave ee?'

— GREAT TRIES 2 —

JONAH LOMU
NEW ZEALAND v ENGLAND
CAPE TOWN, 1995

1   This was not a team score, like Edwards', but a terrifying affirmation that a young giant had entered the rugby world. The only team element to Lomu's great try – scored, like Edwards', in the second minute of the match – was that his New Zealand colleagues did their level best to get him involved from the very first seconds. How they were rewarded! First a kick-off was aimed away from their forwards and into Lomu's follow-up territory. England captain Will Carling fumbled the catch, with Lomu bearing down on him, and New Zealand immediately had an attacking scrum. Their first thrust went right and then, when the move was held up by the English forwards, scrum-half Graeme Bachop flung out a long (some would say untidy) pass to his left. But Bachop knew what he was doing; he wanted the ball in Lomu's hands and, despite it bouncing awkwardly in front of him as he stooped to collect it, the 19-stone wing – who had only turned 20 the month before – safely gathered it up.

2   From a standing start, Lomu tucked the ball under his arm and made for the English line some 40 yards away. Tony Underwood, his opposite wing, was the first to try to stop him. Almost casually, Underwood was made to look like flimsy balsa wood as he was brushed aside with a ramrod handoff.

3   Next to get to Lomu was Carling, covering across, but the skipper's attempted ankle-tap tackle couldn't bring down the juggernaut. It made him stumble slightly, however, but this merely increased the sense of anticipation around the ground as Lomu bore down on England's full back, Mike Catt.

4   The last line of defence, Catt bravely steeled himself. It was as if he wasn't there. Lomu didn't even bother to change direction. He merely trampled all over poor Catt and, with a last triumphant flourish, crashed over the try line like a falling oak to thump the ball down with his left hand. England's players were stunned. Soon, Josh Kronfeld had also scored for New Zealand, and when Lomu ploughed over for what was to be the second of a sensational individual tally of four tries, the All Blacks were 25–0 up with barely a quarter of the match played. This, too, was a World Cup semi-final, a context which provided just another compelling reason why, on that sunlit day in Cape Town, rugby witnessed one of its greatest tries.

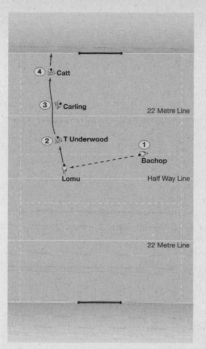

— OLDEST RUGBY CLUBS —

The first official rugby union club was Guy's Hospital Rugby Club, formed in London in 1843, although Arthur Pell's Cambridge University Club (established 1839) was probably the game's oldest. This is disputed, however, by the University of Dublin's Trinity College Rugby Club, who claim to have formed in 1834 (although other sources say that they formed in 1854).

The world's first independent rugby club was founded in 1858, at Blackheath. Rugby Football and Association Football split irrevocably in 1863 when Blackheath and Richmond refused to agree to a ban on running with the ball. The world's longest-running regular rugby union fixture is between Blackheath and Richmond – dating from 1863 – although the two clubs actually first met under 'Harrow rules' in 1861.

WHEN THE FRONT ROW WERE THE
— FIRST TO ARRIVE —

In rugby's early days, there were no specialist positions in the forwards. Scrums, for instance, were organised on a 'first up, first down' basis, whereby the first forwards to arrive at the point where the referee had ordered a scrummage formed the front row. Many early sides, in fact, operated with just a two-man front row, supported by five others around them and an 'eighth man' who chose whether or not to join the scrum, depending on circumstance.

The legendary 1905 All Blacks were perhaps the leading practitioners of the two-man front-row system. British teams soon opted for a three-man front row, yet it was only after the First World War that teams used specialist props and hookers. The 'loose-head' and 'tight-head' propping positions became specialist roles as late as the 1960s, and were due to the increased amount of coaching in the sport and the realisation that the organisation of a forward pack into specialist roles gave added advantage.

— LEWSEY'S PEAKS —

Josh Lewsey, one of England's World Cup winners in 2003, once climbed the three tallest mountains in the British Isles within 24 hours. The London Wasps utility back scaled Ben Nevis in Scotland (at 1,392m the highest peak in Britain), Scafell Pike in the Lake District (978m) and Snowdon in North Wales (1,085m) as a way of raising money for the SANDS (the Stillbirth And Neonatal Death Society). Lewsey accomplished his personal 'three-peaks challenge' in 23 hours and 38 minutes, and raised more than £1,000.

— TBILISI PACKS 'EM IN —

More than 65,000 spectators watched Georgia win their World Cup qualifying clash against Russia at Tbilisi's National Stadium in 2002. The kick-off had to be delayed so that everyone could get in, giving the IRB more proof of the global expansion in interest in the game which simply must be nurtured by the powers-that-be.

— WHAT? NO NICKNAME? —

When a franchise was granted in 2002 for a third professional Scottish district side to be based at Galashiels, in the Borders, chief executive Alistair Cranston immediately asked local rugby fans for ideas about what the new club should be called. Very soon, the almost unanimous answer came back that it should simply be called 'The Borders', which made for a pleasant change in these days of Sharks, Tykes, Warriors and Shoguns and other marketing 'initiatives'. No formal nickname was suggested, either, which says much for the traditional nature of those in Bill McLaren country who love their rugby.

— FATE PLAYS ITS PART —

Chester Williams assumed iconic status in 1995 as the one black player in South Africa's World Cup-winning team. Yet injury had initially caused him to withdraw from the tournament before it began, and he was able to be there at the end only because of the hand of fate.

As with so much about the 1995 World Cup, Williams's presence seemed to have been pre-ordained. The door was re-opened for him by mass brawling during South Africa's final pool game against Canada in Port Elizabeth. Three players – Canadians Gareth Rees and Rod Snow and Springbok hooker James Dalton – were sent off, and two others – Pieter Hendriks of South Africa and Scott Stewart of Canada – were later cited and banned. Hendriks, who had replaced Williams following his hamstring pull in a pre-tournament game, was now on the receiving end of a 60-day suspension.

Despite some queries about whether a banned player should morally be allowed to be replaced, a fit-again Williams was a popular call-up. He made an immediate impact, scoring four tries in the quarter-final victory over Samoa, and by the end of the tournament the much-loved and charismatic Williams had become the living embodiment of what most right-thinking people wanted the new South Africa to be in a non-racial society.

— THE FIELDS OF ATHENRY —

At the great Irish rugby stadiums of Lansdowne Road and Thomond Park these days, there is one song above all others that the crowds of Dublin and Limerick sing. It is also the London Irish club anthem, and so is much in evidence at their home games at the Madejski Stadium in Reading. Even so, it was written as recently as 1985, by the Irish song writer and novelist Pete St John. It is called 'The Fields Of Athenry', and it's not about rugby at all; in fact, the song which has become so associated with the game is about love and exile and recalls the true story of a couple torn apart in County Galway during the Great Famine in Ireland of 1846–52, and runs thus:

> By a lonely prison wall
> I heard a young girl calling,
> 'Michael they are taking you away
> For you stole Trevelyan's corn
> So our young might see the morn
> Now a prison ship lies waiting in the bay.'
>
> Low lie the fields of Athenry
> Where once we watched the
> Small free birds fly.
> Our love was on the wing;
> We had dreams and songs to sing.
> It's lonely round the fields of Athenry.
>
> By that lonely prison wall
> I heard a young man calling,
> 'Nothing matters, Mary, when you're free.
> Against the famine and the Crown,
> I rebelled; they drove me down.
> Now you must raise our child with dignity.'
>
> Low lie the fields of Athenry,
> Where once we watched the
> Small free birds fly.
> Our love was on the wing;
> We had dreams and songs to sing.
> It's lonely round the fields of Athenry.
>
> By a lonely harbour wall,
> She watched the last star falling

As the prison ship sailed out against the sky.
Now she'll live in hope and pray
For her love in Botany Bay.
Oh, it's lonely round the fields of Athenry.

Low lie the fields of Athenry,
Where once we watched the
Small free birds fly.
Our love was on the wing;
We had dreams and songs to sing.
It's lonely round the fields of Athenry.

— RUGBY ACCORDING TO SPIKE —

The great comedian and erstwhile Goon Spike Milligan played
for London Irish B in the late 1930s, before what he always
called 'the bloody war' brought the curtain down on his rugby
career with the club. Later in his life, he and actor Richard
Harris would often turn up together to watch London Irish
matches at Sunbury, and Milligan also wrote the following
personal slant on the rules of rugby for the club's centenary
celebration book:

'Rugby is a game for big buggers; if you're not a big bugger,
you get hurt. I wasn't a big bugger, but I was a fast bugger
and therefore I avoided the big buggers. If I thought I was
going to be tackled by a big 'un, I would drop the ball by
"accident" so that the big bugger couldn't tackle me. Or I
would simply knock on, which would force the referee to
blow his whistle, which would stop the play and therefore
stop the big buggers from tackling this little bugger.
Sometimes, to avoid one of those tackles, I would
"accidentally" step into touch, which would result in a line-
out for more of the big buggers. The small ones were, of
course, not involved!'

— BREAKING NEW GROUND —

New Zealand and Australia met for the 93rd time when they contested the
1991 World Cup semi-final in Dublin, but it was the first match in their long
shared history that had taken place on neutral soil.

— THE FREAK —

'He's a freak and I wish he would go away.' This is what Will Carling said – not entirely in jest – after a Jonah Lomu-inspired New Zealand had beaten England 45–29 in the 1995 World Cup semi-final in Cape Town. Lomu scored four tries, the first after he unforgettably trampled all over Mike Catt following a bulldozing run in which he also brushed aside Tony Underwood and England captain Carling.

— BEER AND RUGBY —

In a purely social sense, beer and rugby go together as naturally as a horse and carriage. The rugby clubhouse on a Saturday night, or the rugby tour, just wouldn't be the same without it. For the professional rugby player, however, the mix is potentially career-damaging. It's simply not possible for the human body to be able to absorb large amounts of alcohol and perform at a peak, either in a training session or a match.

Alcohol affects co-ordination, balance and accuracy, and also slows down reaction times, which for a rugby player translates to not only poor performance but also a greatly increased chance of injury. Strength, power, speed and endurance can also be affected. And it's not just regular drinking that's out of the question; infrequent binge drinking sessions can also have long-term effects on a player's fitness and career.

Drinking alcohol in the immediate recovery period (ie shooting into the bar for a pint or two straight after training or a match) is also frowned upon, as it slows up rehydration and the replacement of depleted fuel stores in the muscles. Therefore, drinking alcohol before properly rehydrating with water and energy drinks in the changing rooms does a player no favours, particularly if he has suffered a slight injury or tissue damage.

— EXPORT OF UK —

Rugby football was taken over the English Channel to France by British wine merchants, who introduced the game to the people of Le Havre in 1872.

— SOMETHING IN THE AIR —

At the end of the 1955 Lions tour of South Africa, several of the British players had firm, written offers of excellent jobs there in their back pockets. Cliff Morgan, one of the stars of the tour, was in great demand, and the flank-forward, DS 'Tug' Wilson, did eventually accept a job offer in Southern Rhodesia. Indeed, there was definitely something about South Africa that caught the eyes of touring British Lions players in general.

In 1968, the Lions included in their party England wing Keith Savage and Irish scrum-half Roger Young. Both subsequently settled in South Africa, and Young is still there to this day, running a dental practice in Cape Town. 'When I came here on that 1968 tour, I quickly realised that so much of this country appealed to me,' he remembers. 'I wanted to move from Ulster, and I have never regretted coming out here to settle. It is a wonderful part of the world in which to live.'

— WORLD CUP FINAL TRY SCORERS —

Only nine players have so far experienced the thrill of scoring a try in a World Cup final. They are:

1987	Michael Jones
	David Kirk
	John Kirwan (New Zealand)
	Pierre Berbizier (France)
1991	Tony Daly (Australia)
1999	Owen Finegan
	Ben Tune (Australia)
2003	Jason Robinson (England)
	Lote Tuqiri (Australia)

— OLLIE'S RECORD —

The English club record for the number of winners' National Cup medals is held by Nigel 'Ollie' Redman of Bath. Redman played in nine of Bath's ten Cup wins during the club's incredible sequence of success from 1984 to 1996. In that time, the only other winners were Harlequins (1988 and 1991) and Leicester (1993).

— JAMIE SALMON —

When Jamie Salmon was capped by England in 1985, he became the first player to have represented New Zealand before doing so. Moreover, Salmon made his England debut against the All Blacks!

— 28 THINGS YOU NEVER KNEW ABOUT — WILL CARLING

After former England captain Will Carling announced his retirement from first-class rugby in 2000, his club, Harlequins, carried the following interview in their official match programme:

1 Corrie or Eastenders?
  Corrie

2 Premiership title or European Cup?
  European Cup

3 Apples or oranges?
  Apples

4 Chinese or Indian food?
  Chinese

5 Dylan Thomas or Bob Dylan?
  Dylan Thomas

6 Lomu or Campese?
  Campese

7 Blonde or brunette?
  Brunette

8 Sean Connery or Roger Moore?
  Sean Connery

9 *Daily Mirror* or looking in the mirror?
  Neither!

10 Monarchy or Republic?
  Monarchy

11 Formula One or Indy Cars?
  Formula One

12 DIY or don't ask me?
Don't ask me

13 *The Simpsons* or *South Park*?
The Simpsons

14 Are you a dancer or a wallflower?
Wallflower

15 Euro or sterling?
Euro

16 Jerry Springer or Oprah?
Jerry Springer

17 Armani or Versace?
Armani

18 Denise Richards or Denise Van Outen?
Denise Van Outen

19 Parkinson or Alan Partridge?
Partridge

20 Vic or Bob?
Vic

21 Tony Blair or Lionel Blair?
Lionel Blair

22 World Cup every two years or four?
Four

23 Deep pan or thin and crispy?
Thin & crispy

24 Read the book or watch the video?
Read the book

25 Christmas or New Year?
Christmas

26 Golf clubs or night clubs?
Golf clubs

27 *Friends* or *Seinfeld*?
Friends

28 Premiership or British League?
British League

— WHAT'S WRONG WITH JAM? —

The mix of players for the 1955 Lions tour was extraordinary, and included Welsh miners, Scottish farmers, Irish labourers, English City of London financiers and Cambridge University students, to cite but a few. One of them, Pontypool and Wales prop-forward Ray Prosser, was a steelworker who had never been exposed to such a breathtaking array of men with differing backgrounds. One day, complaining at something said by the Harlequins England and former Cambridge University lock-forward, RWD Marques, Prosser exclaimed, 'There 'e goes again, always using long bloomin' words like marmalade.'

— FIJIAN SUNRISE —

The first rugby match to be played in Fiji took place in 1884, between European and Fijian soldiers of the Native Constabulary. The Fijian Rugby Union was formed in 1913 – mostly for players with European backgrounds – and a Native Rugby Union followed in 1915 for Fiji-born players. The two unions didn't merge until 1945. Fiji's first overseas match – against a Samoan side in Apia – began at 7am so that the home payers could still go to work afterwards. Legend has it that the pitch had a large tree growing in the middle of it.

— WELSH ALL BLACKS —

Neath Rugby Club – now amalgamated with Swansea to form the Neath–Swansea Ospreys – were always known as the Welsh All Blacks because of their black attire. This originated, it is believed, as a mark of sorrow and respect when a player called Dick Gordon died from injuries sustained during a match against Bridgend in 1880.

— KEEPING UP WITH THE JONESES —

There have always been plenty of players called Williams, Jones, Davies and Thomas in Wales teams over the years, but in early November 2004 the Welsh selectors made history by naming no fewer than six Joneses in their XV to play against South Africa at the Millennium Stadium.

Wales had fielded five Joneses during the 2003 World Cup, in a match against Italy, and a quintet of Davieses versus Scotland in 1939, but this preponderance of similarly named players was breaking new ground. Stephen Jones, the former Llanelli fly-half, was the only Jones selected in the back line; the five Jones boys in the pack were made up of the entire front row: Adam and Duncan at prop and Steve at hooker, plus Dafydd at blindside flanker and Ryan at number eight.

— KNOCKOUT —

A rugby-playing policeman once knocked himself out when involved in a search of a clothes shop in the Wirral, Merseyside. He thought he saw an intruder, dived to rugby tackle him and hit a long mirror headfirst.

— SINNERS TO SAINTS —

The name of Northampton Saints Rugby Football Club has its origins in a Christian youth club for problem children formed in 1880 by the Reverend Samuel Wathen Wigg, who saw the game of rugby union as being an ideal vehicle for keeping them in check.

— THE NORTHERN SPLIT —

The breakaway from the RFU by 22 northern clubs in 1895 – to form the Northern Rugby Union – led to the creation of rugby league and 100 years of acrimony in relations between the two forms of the game.

From 1879, a one-shilling (5p) expense had been allowed for those playing in international matches, and later it was also permitted for players to claim travel expenses for away matches. Payment for loss of earnings was not allowed. From 1888, however, the northern clubs mounted a campaign for 'broken time' allowances to be paid to compensate for money lost while playing rugby. This was a particularly relevant argument because the bulk of the England team was made up of players from Yorkshire and Lancashire, with the former team having won the county championship every year bar one (when Lancashire won) from the tournament's inauguration in 1889 until the Great Split of 1895.

Matters came to a head in 1893 when a meeting at the Westminster Palace Hotel in London debated the following proposal from JA Miller, a representative of Yorkshire: 'That players be allowed compensation for *bona fide* loss of time.'

G Rowland Hill, the secretary of the RFU and the most powerful figure in rugby in that era, moved the following amendment: 'That this meeting, believing that the above principle is contrary to the true interests of the game and its spirit, declines to sanction the same.' Amid heated scenes, after what was a tense and fractious occasion, this amendment was carried by 146 votes, but 120 of those votes were proxies, gathered in before the meeting had even taken place.

Initially, the northern clubs wanted to stay within the RFU, and the split occurred only two years later when R Cail, the RFU president, further tightened the laws relating to professionalism. This convinced the northerners that they would never receive fair treatment from the south-dominated RFU, and a meeting of 20 clubs at the George Hotel in Huddersfield on 28 August 1895 led to the formation of the Northern Rugby Union. This had a noticeable impact on the fortunes of the England national team; standards dropped so much that it wasn't until 1910 that England again won the International Championship. Also, in the ten years following the Great Split, the number of clubs affiliated to the RFU halved.

— DEANO —

'There he was, half his teeth missing, cheekbones smashed, hair all over the place, his skin looking as if it hadn't seen the sun for six months. He looked as if he'd just come out of a bunker. But what a player.'
– Laurent Cabannes, the France back-row forward,
on England number eight Dean Richards

— THE RISE OF COMPETITION ABROAD —

South Africa's domestic provincial competition, the Currie Cup, was introduced as early as 1901, when an all-conquering British touring side awarded the trophy – made by the Castle Shipping Line – to their hardest opponents, Griqualand West. Meanwhile, in New Zealand, the Ranfurly Shield was first competed for in 1904, having been awarded to an unbeaten Auckland side the previous year. The Shield was a challenge competition, and Wellington were the first winners when they were successful by 6–3 against Auckland.

— RECORD SIGNING —

The £1 million that Sir John Hall's Newcastle club paid to Wigan Rugby League Club in 1997 for the transfer of Va'aiga Tuigamala remains rugby union's most expensive signing.

— BIGGEST TOUR —

A New Zealand side calling themselves 'the Maoris' undertook the biggest rugby tour of all time in 1888. They played 107 matches in all: 74 of them in 25 weeks in Britain, and then additional games in Australia and against other New Zealand sides.

— JOHN ALLAN —

Between 1991 and 1994, hooker John Allan played Tests against England for both South Africa and Scotland.

— THE RUGBY FIELD —

The field on which rugby is played should be no more
than 100m in length and 70m in width. The depth
of the in-goal area should be no more than 22m.

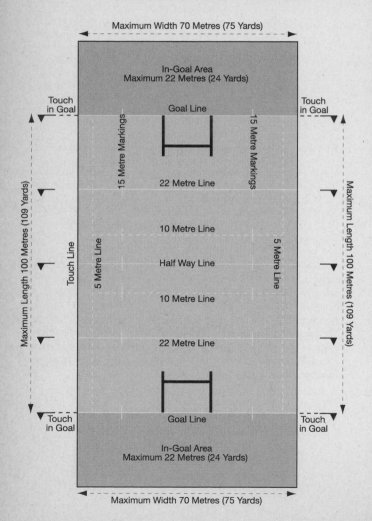

— THE TRIPLE CROWN —

This is a mythical trophy 'awarded' to one of the four home nations for defeating the other three in the International Championship. This is why, in modern times, it has been possible for England (or Scotland) to have the Calcutta Cup, the Triple Crown, the Grand Slam and the Six Nations Championship all at stake in one match.

— RUFFIANS? —

Rugby was once described as 'a game for ruffians played by gentlemen'. It has often been said since that soccer is the exact opposite.

— SEVENS RUGBY —

Seven-a-side rugby is (usually) played with three forwards and four backs, on a full-sized pitch, and games last typically for seven minutes per half. It is fast, furious, and demands huge fitness levels of its players. Most unions around the world use sevens rugby – and specifically the IRB-run World Sevens series – as a development theatre for their up-and-coming international-class players.

Jonah Lomu was a classic product of sevens rugby on the international stage, as it aided his development from a teenage back-row forward into one of the outstanding wings of all time.

A young Lawrence Dallaglio was a member of the England sevens team that won the inaugural World Cup Sevens tournament in 1993. England beat Australia 21–17 in the final and, ten years later, Dallaglio was a World Cup winner at full 15-a-side level, too, when England beat the Wallabies by an almost identical score.

— STRANGE BUT TRUE —

Frenchman André Behoteguy wore a beret while playing his 19 internationals between 1923 and 1929; Basil McLear, who represented Ireland from 1905 to 1907, wore white gloves; and Joe Simpson wore glasses when he played for Wales in 1884.

— THE LIONS' ROAR —

In 1974, the British Lions took the Welsh hooker Bobby Windsor to South Africa as a member of their touring party. 'The Duke', as he was known, was a true man of the Welsh valleys, perfectly at home at the bottom of a ferocious maul with half a dozen fellow Welshmen punching and kicking the living daylights out of him. But when it came to leaving his own patch, Windsor was less certain of himself.

During that Lions tour, a few days were found for them to travel to the Kruger National Park and go out driving each day, looking for animals. The players were all accommodated in individual *rondavels*, round thatched huts that provided beds for three players.

One night, after a long evening around the camp fire, most of the players decided to turn in. Windsor, nervous and never quite sure what might be lurking around the corner, kept close to his room-mates as they found their way back through the dark to their rondavel. Eventually, the lights went out and all was quiet.

The peace was shattered by a sudden roaring sound outside the window of the small building. Windsor was in his bed, shaking with fear, and enquiring of his room-mates which animal it might be that had broken into the camp.

The roaring continued for a moment, and was then immediately followed by an almighty crash as something large came through the window. 'The Duke' was so frightened that he leapt out of bed and was heading for one of his fellow player's beds to climb in, when he felt something sinister on his foot. It was covered with fur.

Without further ado, Windsor lashed out, grabbing the furry animal and kicking it to shreds. Finally, he picked it up and hurled it against the wall just to make sure he had finished it off.

He'd done that, all right. When the light was turned on, Windsor's room-mates looked in astonishment at what remained of the soft, cuddly lion that had been the team's mascot: Windsor had kicked and ripped it into pieces. Beside it, meanwhile, lay a huge log that had come through the window, and outside could be heard the sounds of men groaning as three of the other Lions players tried to suppress their roaring laughter.

— BATH'S WINNING CAPTAINS —

The seven Bath captains who lifted the English Cup during the club's astonishing run of ten wins out of ten Twickenham final appearances from 1984 to 1996 were Roger Spurrell, John Palmer, Richard Hill, Stuart Barnes, Andy Robinson, John Hall and Phil de Glanville.

— THREE UNLIKELY RUGBY PLAYERS —

Proof that rugby union is truly a global game for all comes with the knowledge that former US President Bill Clinton, Pope John Paul II and former Ugandan dictator Idi Amin are among those who have played the game. Clinton was introduced to the game while a Rhodes Scholar at Oxford University, playing at lock, and he also represented the Little Rock RFC in his home town in Arkansas. Pope John Paul, meanwhile, was an accomplished player in his youth, representing his native Poland at international level, and Idi Amin was an official reserve when the East African team played the touring British Lions in 1955.

— THE LOCAL DERBY —

The regional variations of football played for centuries in the British Isles often flew in the face of what authority might have wanted. In the 1300s, 1400s and 1500s there were a total of nine European monarchs who decreed it an offence to play 'foote balle'. Archery was deemed to be a more noteworthy and valuable pastime, and punishments for those caught playing football ranged from fines to imprisonment.

However, increased participation in sport by the masses followed James I's Declaration of Sports in 1618, which encouraged the playing of games on Sundays. In a forerunner to how quickly rugby football became so popular with the masses in the 1800s, the long-evolved former medieval version of football was soon a feature of Sundays and holidays around Britain. Shrove Tuesday became a notorious football-playing day in many areas of the country, and the annual match at Derby was so bloody and infamous that its memory lives on in the phrase 'local derby', implying a fierce struggle between traditional close rivals.

— TERMINOLOGY —

Rugby, like all sports, has an accepted terminology for all that happens on the field of play. Here, in alphabetical order, is a selection of rugby terms:

- **Advantage Line** – An imaginary line that extends across the field from where the last scrum, ruck, maul, line-out or play of the ball was formed. Often also called the 'gain line'.

- **Against The Head** – Nowadays, a rare instance of the ball being hooked back by the opposition after a scrummage put-in.

- **Ankle Tap** – A method of bringing down a player by touching his ankle and unbalancing him. This must be done with the hand. Tripping with the boot or leg is not allowed.

- **Blind Side** – The opposite side of the field to where the backs line up when there is a scrum, line-out, ruck or maul.

- **Charge Down** – The blocking of an opponent's kick with the hands, arms or body. If the ball subsequently touches the ground, it is not penalised as a knock-on.

- **Drop-out** – A method of restarting play either from the 22m line or the centre spot by means of a drop kick.

- **Dummy** – A move whereby a player pretends to pass the ball to another player, but instead keeps possession of it.

- **Fair Catch** – When a player catches the ball when stationary and with both feet on the ground, on his own side of the 22m line, and catches the ball cleanly from a kick, knock-on or throw-forward by an opponent, he is deemed to have made a fair catch and can call 'mark'. A free kick is then awarded.

- **Forward Pass** – Self-explanatory, but officially called a 'throw forward' in the laws.

- **Garryowen** – An 'up and under' high kick named after a famous Irish club side who were well known for the tactic.

- **Grubber** – A kick of the ball that causes it to roll along the ground, usually bouncing awkwardly for a defender.

- **Hand-off** – A method of fending off a tackler by pushing him away with an open hand.

- **Knock-on** – This occurs when a ball bounces forward off the hand or arm of a player attempting to catch it or pick it up. Play can continue, however, if the ball bounces sideways or backwards.

- **Line Of Touch** – An imaginary line in the field of play at right angles to the touch line through the place where the ball is to be thrown in at a line-out.

- **Line-outs** – An arrangement whereby two sets of forwards stand parellel to each other. They must not be in front of the 5m line or behind the 15m line when the throw-in is made. Players must also be standing 2m apart when the ball is thrown in. The maximum number of players in a line-out is determined by the side throwing in, thus there can be a 'shortened line-out' of a minimum of two players.

- **Mark** – The place on the pitch where the free kick or penalty kick is awarded. Alternatively, the term is used when a player makes a call of 'mark' and takes a fair catch.

- **Maul** – A scrimmage of players from both teams around the player carrying the ball. If he or the ball drops to the ground then the maul becomes a ruck.

- **Pack** – Collective name for the eight forwards.

- **Penalty Try** – A try awarded at the referee's discretion if a player is fouled or obstructed when a try would probably have resulted. All conversions of penalty tries are taken from a position directly in front of the goalposts.

- **Scrum** – At least five players from each side must form a scrummage. It is a means of restarting play, usually following an infringement. Both sets of forwards must interlock legally and properly, and the side putting in the ball, and winning it, must use the ball positively or risk the referee deciding to reset the scrum and award possession to the other side. Also, if a scrum is wheeled legally by more than 90 degrees, the opposing side get the put-in to a reset scrum.

- **Set Piece** – A scrum or line-out.

- **Tap Kick** – A kick of a few inches made after a restart by a player to himself. He can then either run the ball, pass it or kick it.

- **Tight Five** – A collective name for the three front-row forwards and the two second-row (lock) forwards.

- **Tight-head** – The number-three prop forward, who packs down at the scrum with his head between the opposition loose-head prop and hooker. The tight-head prop is the cornerstone of a pack at scrum time.

- **Touchdown** – This is NOT a try, but occurs when a defending player grounds the ball inside his own in-goal area. If he has carried the ball into his own in-goal area, a 5m scrum to the other side is awarded. If the ball

— TERMINOLOGY (CONT'D) —

has already been propelled into the in-goal area by an opponent, a drop-out is awarded.

- **Touch-in Goal** – Awarded when the ball goes out of play behind the in-goal area.

— GONE FOR A BURTON —

Gloucester prop Mike Burton was the first England player to be sent off. He was given his marching orders by Australian referee Bob Burnett during the 1975 second Test against Australia in Brisbane following a late tackle.

— A WORLD CUP WINNERS' XV —

15	Matt Burke (Australia, 1999)
14	John Kirwan (New Zealand, 1987)
13	Dan Herbert (Australia, 1999)
12	Tim Horan (Australia, 1991 and 1999)
11	David Campese (Australia, 1991)
10	Jonny Wilkinson (England, 2003)
9	Joost van der Westhuizen (South Africa, 1995)
1	Steve McDowell (New Zealand, 1987)
2	Sean Fitzpatrick (New Zealand, 1987)
3	Os du Randt (South Africa, 1995)
4	Martin Johnson (England 2003, captain)
5	John Eales (Australia, 1991 and 1999)
6	Richard Hill (England, 2003)
7	Michael Jones (New Zealand, 1987)
8	Wayne Shelford (New Zealand, 1987)

Replacements: Jason Robinson (England, 2003)
Michael Lynagh (Australia, 1991)
George Gregan (Australia, 1999)
Phil Vickery (England, 2003)
Phil Kearns (Australia, 1991)
Mark Andrews (South Africa, 1995)
Willy Ofahengaue (Australia, 1991)

— WINDSOR'S HOSPITAL PASS —

Injured British Lions players in South Africa could never expect much sympathy if they got carted off to hospital. On the Lions' 1955 tour, one of the Lions had to have a small operation, and when he came round from the anaesthetic he found a certain part of his body had been painted in the colours of the host nation.

Another player who found an unsympathetic medical fraternity was the Welsh hooker Bobby Windsor on the 1974 tour. He was taken ill on the plane flying from London, probably because of something he had eaten at the airport before departure. By the time the plane had touched down in Johannesburg, he was decidedly rough and had to be taken to a local hospital, where he was detained for a few days. 'The next morning, when the doc came to see me,' said Windsor later, 'the first thing he said was, "You've got a case of Bok fever. It's a common enough complaint among visiting rugby men in this part of the world. I think it's to do with fear at what our boys might be about to do to you."' Windsor and his fellow Lions had the last laugh, though, winning the Test series 3–0, with one drawn, and finishing their tour unbeaten.

TENDING FOR THE SICK

British Lions getting sick in South Africa, meanwhile, usually found themselves being overwhelmed by hospitality. When the former Welsh back-row man RCC (Clem) Thomas was taken ill with appendicitis on the Lions' 1955 tour of South Africa, he was rushed off to the local hospital in Kimberley. Thomas had his operation but was forced to stay in the hospital for a week. By the end of that time, he reported, his private ward was filled with boxes of chocolates, crates of beer and dozens of cartons of cigarettes.

Thomas had a hotter than hot reception when he finally recovered his fitness and made it back onto the playing field, but he never forgot that warmest of warm welcomes from the local people in Kimberley.

— HOW THE LEGEND OF THE ALL BLACKS BEGAN —

The first All Blacks tour of Britain was in 1905, and the New Zealanders lost only one of their 32 matches, scoring 55 points (a remarkable tally for the time) against Devon, then the reigning county champions. The English county championship had been launched in 1889, and was long regarded as being the second most important tournament in England after the International Championship. The first All Blacks tourists therefore made a huge impact on the consciousness of British rugby fans, especially with the technique, pace and power of their play, and this significant first impression was built upon massively by the second All Blacks tour of 1924, on which they won all 28 of their matches, scoring a total of 650 points.

However, it was the 1905 tour, by the 'Originals', that laid out the legend of All Blacks domination. The embryonic Lions side of 1888 lost two of the their New Zealand matches – to Taranaki and Auckland – and the New Zealanders' flair for the game was further emphasised by the epic 1888/9 New Zealand natives' tour of Britain, Australia and New Zealand, during which they beat Ireland during their long stay in the British Isles.

New Zealand played Australia for the first time in 1903, winning 22–3, and in 1904 won a Test against a touring British side. By 1905, the New Zealand side was well established as a leading power in the game, and in captain Dave Gallaher and vice-captain Billy Stead the team had visionary players and notable authorities on the tactics and technical requirements needed for successful innovation. Gallaher himself, who perished in the First World War, played as a wing forward, or 'rover', which was a position unknown in Britain at the time and which contributed to the spectacular impression his team made on their travels.

The 1905 All Blacks used planned and pre-arranged moves, such as splitting a line-out and catapulting a wing through the gap created. On their tour the All Blacks scored 33 tries from line-outs, turning on its head an aspect of the game previously seen as merely a restart vehicle. They also used specialists in certain positions, code words at pre-arranged set moves, miss-moves in the back division, dummy runners, quick balls from rucks (or 'loose scrummages', as they were known then) and employed a predominantly fast running game that ignored the common British tactic of mainly kicking to touch. These really were new techniques, and the 1905 All Blacks – who lost only one match, due to a hotly disputed disallowed try by Bob Deans against Wales in Cardiff – can be seen as the true fathers of modern rugby.

— RUGBY OFFICIALS —

Neutral referees were used for the first time in 1881, with touch judges being introduced at international level in 1889.

— RUGBY'S DEBT TO THE SCHOOLS —

It wasn't just Rugby School that spawned the game of rugby football; English public schools in general share much of the responsibility for the transformation of the popular medieval football game into a more organised, acceptable sport.

Winchester College began to play a round-ball version of football in 1647, thus giving it much-needed respectability at a crucial stage of history, and soon most of the leading schools in England were playing their own, similar versions of the game. At Eton College a wall-less form of football was played for almost 50 years before the wall was constructed in 1717, which led to the famous Eton wall game being invented. Meanwhile, a form of football similar to modern-day Australian-rules football was played at Rugby School for almost a century before William Webb Ellis was a pupil.

It's fortunate that the game took off in the schools, because football for the common man in the streets and fields of Britain became increasingly suppressed by the local authorities from 1750. Indeed, in 1835 the Highways Act forbade the playing of football on public land, and it was a law that was upheld vigorously by special constables and dragoons.

— WOMEN'S RUGBY GAINS GLOBAL AUDIENCE —

The USA won the inaugural Women's World Cup in 1991, beating England in the final at Cardiff Arms Park by 19–6.

— GARETH EDWARDS' BOYHOOD —

'Growing up in Wales meant two things to me: rugby on Saturday and chapel on Sunday. The thought of doing anything else just never crossed our minds as youngsters.'

— THURSDAY CURTAIN-RAISER —

It's a strange fact, but a true one, that the first international match ever played by a touring British Isles side was on a Thursday. It took place in Port Elizabeth, South Africa, on 30 July 1891, between the home nation and a British Isles side captained by Bill Maclagan, of Edinburgh Academicals and Scotland.

The British team won 4–0 and went on to win the three-match international series 3–0, finishing their tour with 20 wins out of 20 matches. Yet, when that 1891 British Isles team first arrived in South Africa, they had little idea of what to expect. The Boer War had not yet been fought, and the vast country was of seemingly endless size, when it came to travel. The party found itself being pulled by horse-drawn carriages and 'Cape carts', as they were known, for several hours, or even a day or two, from one destination to another. They are said to have amused themselves during the long, bumpy and uncomfortable overland journeys by attempting to catch wild monkeys along the way. At one overnight stop, it was said that sleeping accommodation was so restricted that five of the touring British squad had to share the same bed.

The team travelled all over the country, visiting towns or cities such as Cape Town, Kimberley, Port Elizabeth, Pietermaritzburg, Johannesburg and Stellenbosch. They sailed from England on 20 June and arrived home at the end of September.

Interestingly, only players from England and Scotland were chosen for the pioneering tour, although in 1888 one Welshman – WH Thomas, of Cambridge University and Wales – had been selected for the first-ever official visit by a British team overseas, to Australia and New Zealand.

— THE LONGEST JOURNEY —

The 1888 British rugby party travelled far and wide. They started with nine games in New Zealand before moving on to Australia, for the major part of the tour. In subsequent years, of course, British Lions sides tended to do it the other way round, when New Zealand rugby was much stronger than its Australian counterpart in the 1950s and 1960s. The British then played 16 matches in Australia before sailing back to New Zealand to play another ten games.

The team had departed from England by sea on 8 March 1888 and played its first tour match on 28 April. Its last game was on 3 October, and the party arrived home, after another long boat journey, on 11 November after an extraordinary journey lasting 35 weeks and three days. They took just 22 players but, in all, played 35 matches. A Lancastrian from the Swinton club, H Eagles, achieved the extraordinary feat of playing in every single one of those 35 matches, of which the British side won 27 and lost only two.

— BIGGEST KICK —

The record for the longest successful penalty kick in rugby is held by Ernie Cooper, who was a 17-year-old schoolboy at the time. While playing for Bridlington School against an army XV in 1944, Cooper toe-ended the ball through the posts and over the bar from just outside his own team's 25-yard line. The distance from where the penalty was taken to the nearest goalpost was 81 yards, according to the referee, who measured it immediately after the game with a chain usually used by the school to check the length of javelin throws.

'There was none of that round-the-corner nonsense in those days,' said Cooper recently. 'It was all about momentum and a great connection. I was a big lad for 17, and I ran up hard and straight and wellied it with the reinforced toe-end of my boot. My foot ended up somewhere around my head, but the ball just kept going and going. It didn't just creep over. It landed behind the dead-ball line.'

The Guinness Book Of Records also records that the longest distance for a successful penalty kick in international rugby is the 70 yards and eight and a half inches achieved by Wales full back Paul Thorburn against Scotland in 1986.

— THE SIX MOST SUCCESSFUL ENGLAND CAPTAINS —

Name	Tenure	Success Rate (%)	Won	Drew	Lost
WJA ('Dave') Davies	1913–23	91	10	1	0
Martin Johnson	1998–2003	87	34	0	5
Will Carling	1988–97	75	44	1	14
Eric Evans	1948–58	69	9	2	2
Wavell Wakefield	1920-27	54	7	2	4
Bill Beaumont	1975–82	52	11	2	8

— JONATHAN THE FIRST —

When Jonathan Davies quit rugby union for the lure of a professional rugby-league contract to play in the north of England in late 1988, he was doing merely what scores of fellow Welshmen had done in the 90 years or so since the Great Split of 1895. But when Davies then greeted the onset of the professional era in rugby union in 1995 by moving back to Cardiff in a £90,000 deal, he became the first former union man to be transferred back across rugby's Rubicon.

— TRI-NATIONS SERIES WINNERS —

The Tri-Nations is the southern hemisphere's answer to the commercially successful Five/Six Nations Championship. It was conceived during the 1995 World Cup and launched as a central feature of the three top southern hemisphere unions' initial ten-year £340 million television deal with Rupert Murdoch's News Corporation. Here are the tournament winners over the last nine years:

1996	New Zealand
1997	New Zealand
1998	South Africa
1999	New Zealand
2000	Australia
2001	Australia
2002	New Zealand
2003	New Zealand
2004	South Africa

— BOW TIES AND CHAMPAGNE —

In 1990 the final of the French Club Championship was won by Racing Club de France and was the first domestic title for this aristocratic club since 1959. To mark the occasion, the Racing backs decided to wear bow ties and berets, and at half-time the whole team sipped champagne out on the field. But this was no stroll to victory; opponents Agen took Racing to extra time before style was wedded to glory.

— TOP 20 MOST INTERNATIONAL POINTS* —

1	Neil Jenkins (Wales)	1,049 (87 matches)
2	Diego Dominguez (Italy)	983 (74)
3	Andrew Mehrtens (New Zealand)	967 (70)
4	Michael Lynagh (Australia)	911 (72)
5	Matthew Burke (Australia)	878 (81)
6	Jonny Wilkinson (England)	817 (52)
7	Gavin Hastings (Scotland)	667 (61)
8	Grant Fox (New Zealand)	645 (46)
9	Nicky Little (Fiji)	574 (53)
10	Hugo Porta (Argentina)	529 (57)
11	David Humphreys (Ireland)	511 (65)
12	Gareth Rees (Canada)	487 (55)
13	Gonzalo Quesada (Argentina)	486 (38)
14	Stefano Bettarello (Italy)	483 (55)
15	Ronan O'Gara (Ireland)	465 (47)
16	Bobby Ross (Canada)	419 (58)
17	Percy Montgomery (South Africa)	415 (61)
18	Paul Grayson (England)	400 (32)
19	Rob Andrew (England)	396 (71)
20	Stephen Jones (Wales)	384 (43)

* As at 1 January 2005

— LINEEN THE SCOT —

Sean Lineen, the centre who played in Scotland's 1990 Grand Slam team and 29 times in all for his 'country', was later found to have no Scottish blood in him at all. He's a 100 per cent New Zealander, besides which his father, Terry, actually played 12 times for the All Blacks.

— FROM RUSSIA WITH NO LOVE LOST —

Llanelli are a small-town club from West Wales who are big on achievement. Many times Welsh club champions and cup winners, they also beat Australia in 1908 and 1992, and in 1972 – and most famously of all – the New Zealand All Blacks. But in 1957 Welsh international lock Rhys Williams led a Llanelli side to the final of the World Youth Games in Moscow, and the game against Romanian team Grivita Rosie was so violent and bad-tempered that the Soviet authorities banned rugby from being played in the USSR for almost 30 years.

— JOHNSON ON WOODWARD —

'Clive had lots of ideas. The terrible ones were dropped, the good ones adapted and the great ones we used.'

– Martin Johnson on Sir Clive Woodward.

— AUSTRALIA'S COMING OF AGE —

The British Lions didn't make a proper, in-depth tour of Australia for 30 years after the 1959 Lions went there and played six matches *en route* to heading over the Tasman Sea for what was considered the major part of the trip, in New Zealand. In the intervening years, Australian rugby was regarded as not being strong enough to justify a major Lions visit. However, by 1989 things had changed, and the Scottish wing-forward Finlay Calder led the Lions on an historic first tour of Australia in its own right.

As if to point out to the Lions what they'd been missing, and how unjustified their 30-year absence had been, the Australians promptly walloped the Lions 30–12 in the first Test, in Sydney. It was a major shock for everyone involved in British rugby, even though it was generally known that Australia had become one of the strong sides of world rugby, following their 1984 Grand Slam tour of the British Isles.

Calder's Lions knew they had to dig deep to get a foothold on the three-match Test series, but unfortunately they went a mite too far. The second Test in Brisbane was marked by a series of punch-ups and fist-fights, the use of boots and flying bodies hurling themselves into the fray. The scenes were ugly and deserved no place on a Lions tour, but the Lions made their point in so physical a contest, beating the Australians 19–12 to set up a series decider in Sydney the following week.

That decider for the rubber was an even tighter affair, although happily it didn't contain the further flare-ups that many had predicted. Come full time, the Lions scraped in with a 19–18 victory to win the series 2–1. Even so, the manner of the outcome proved conclusively that Australian rugby was never again likely to be downgraded in terms of the viability of Lions tours.

— WORLD CUP VENUES: AUSTRALASIA —

— FRANCE OUTLAWED —

In 1931, France were kicked out of the International Championship due to their top clubs paying players. A communiqué from the Home Unions Committee included the following words: 'After examination of the documentary evidence…we are compelled to state that, owing to the unsatisfactory state of the game of Rugby Football in France, neither our Union, nor the Clubs or Unions under its jurisdiction, will be able to arrange or fulfil fixtures with France or French clubs until we are satisfied that conduct of the game has been placed on a satisfactory basis in all essentials.' The penalty, internationally, for this perceived professionalism was expulsion from the championship until 1947.

— THE COOK ISLANDS' FAMOUS SONS —

The Cook Islands might be only specks of land in the vast Pacific Ocean, but nevertheless they produced former Australian rugby-league captain Mal Meninga and New Zealand's All Blacks brothers Graeme and Stephen Bachop.

— ROMANIA'S PRIDE BEFORE THE FALL —

In the 1980s there was a strong case for including Romania in an expanded Six Nations Championship: rugby had been strong in the country since the 1950s and the national side was powerful enough to beat Scotland in 1984 and 1991, Wales in 1983 and 1988 and France in 1990. But the revolution against the dictator Nicolae Ceauscescu not only cost Romanian rugby the life of its former national captain, flanker Florica Murariu, but also disrupted the sport extremely badly. Italy's progress in the 1990s saw them leapfrog ahead of Romania and win a coveted place at the Six Nations table instead in 2000.

— A GAME OF LIFE AND DEATH —

Armand Vacquerin was a bull-like prop forward who won 26 caps for France in the 1970s and was a fully paid-up member of a fearsome Béziers pack that dominated – and intimidated – French club rugby in that era. In 1993, however, Vacquerin killed himself when he walked into a bar and decided to play an individual game of Russian Roulette with a pistol after no one there would play against him.

— RUGBY'S KAMIKAZE PILOT —

The highly popular former president of the Japanese Rugby Union, Shiggy Konno, who was educated in Britain, often used to tell the story of how he would have become one of his country's last kamikaze pilots but for the fact that his plane ran out of fuel.

— VERNON PUGH —

The late Vernon Pugh, QC, was chairman of the IRB when rugby union finally embraced professionalism in August 1995. This is what he said four years later, when much of the dust of that cataclysmic event had settled:

'There was no alternative to embracing professionalism. People were being paid on a concealed basis in some countries, or more openly in others. That had to be addressed.

'The demands on the players was another factor. If we were asking athletes to perform at the intensity and frequency that we were in 1993 and 1994, then it was totally unfair to do so without recompense.

You couldn't have the upside of commercial growth, worldwide involvement and expansion everywhere without the necessary corollary of some of the money going to those that generated it most.

'We also had to take account of some of the other issues which were causing concern at the time. The southern hemisphere Newscorp deal gave Australia, New Zealand and South Africa the benefit of huge amounts of money, some of which would have been placed in so-called development funds to pay their players. Suddenly half the world would have had a group of very well-paid players, whereas the other half would not, and that would have led to a split game, with the northern hemisphere very vulnerable to attack from entrepreneurs.

'As it was, after the 1995 World Cup, I had 60 contracts of Europe's top players scattered across my living room floor, all of whom had committed to an unauthorised professional rugby circus.'

— LA MARSEILLAISE —

Allons enfants de la Patrie,
Le jour de gloire est arrivé!
Contre nous de la tyrannie!
L'étendard sanglant est levé (bis)
Entendez-vous dans nos campagnes
Mugir ces feroces soldats?
Ils viennent jusque dans vos bras
Égorger vos fils, vos compagnes.

Aux armes citoyens!
Formez vos bataillons!
Marchons, marchons
Qu'un sang impur
Abreuve nos sillons.

— FIVE MORE FAMOUS RUGBY NICKNAMES —

Pitbull – Brian Moore
The Fun Bus – Jason Leonard
The Clamp – Allan Bateman
Ollie – Nigel Redman
The Barrel – Stuart Barnes

— FASTEST TRY —

When Tom Voyce, the London Wasps wing, pounced on a dropped catch by Will Greenwood – from the kick-off – and crossed the Harlequins line on the evening of 5 November 2004, it officially became the fastest try scored in British rugby union history. Voyce's score was timed at coming after just 9.63 seconds of the Zurich Premiership match. The world record at that stage for the quickest international try was held by Scotland flanker John Leslie, whose 10.8-second effort came for the Scots against Wales at Murrayfield in 1999.

— THE EXILES —

Historically, London Irish, London Welsh and London Scottish have all been leading clubs on the English scene. All three have provided their 'home' nations with a steady stream of players, and in 1971 the British Lions drew on five London Welsh players, including the captain, John Dawes.

In the professional era, however, only London Irish have thrived. Scottish went bankrupt and forfeited its position in the professional structure, before being re-founded as an amateur club playing in the London leagues, while Welsh have slipped down the divisions almost apologetically. Other exile clubs in the English capital city are London New Zealand, London French, London Cornish, London Maoris and London Japanese.

— TWO OFF —

Geoff Wheel, of Wales, and Willie Duggan, of Ireland, will forever be bracketed together in the record books. In 1977, they provided the first instance of two players being sent off in the same international. The game's referee was Norman Sanson.

— ENGLISH ANAGRAMS —

Neil Back and Nick Beal played together in England's 1999 World Cup quarter-final defeat against South Africa (amongst other occasions). Their names are mutual anagrams.

— HERE'S TO YOU, MR ROBINSON —

Jason Robinson became the first former rugby league player to captain England when he led the side against Canada at Twickenham in November 2004. Robinson, nicknamed 'Billy Whizz' for his idiosyncratic running style, scored 13 tries in 20 rugby league internationals for Great Britain and England during his distinguished club career with Wigan. Following a brief initial foray with Bath in the late 1990s, he opted to swap codes permanently when he signed for Sale in 2000. He also scored England's only try in the 2003 World Cup final victory against Australia.

— BOOTS ON...AND OFF —

Fiji's international side wore boots for the first time in 1938, to mark the arrival of the New Zealand Maoris for their inaugural tour of the island. However, several players discarded their boots as the match progressed.

— ERIC LIDDELL —

The 'Chariots of Fire' runner, who won the 400m gold medal in the 1924 Paris Olympics, was also a successful wing three-quarter for Scotland. His great pace brought him three tries in the seven internationals he played before he retired from senior sport in 1925, aged 23, to answer his calling to do missionary work in China. Liddell made his Scotland rugby debut at the Stade Colombes, where he was to win Olympic gold 18 months later, and he was still two weeks short of his 20th birthday when he played against France on 2 January 1922. He remains the only rugby international to have also won an individual Olympic title.

— HONORARY WELSHMAN —

It was 1976 before a non-Welshman played for the London Welsh first XV. He was Neil Bennett, an Englishman.

— THE BARBARIANS —

Founded in 1890, the Barbarians are a club with no permanent home, no ground and no clubhouse, and they traditionally conduct all their business by post. If an invitation to represent the Baa-Baas drops through your letterbox, however, it is considered to be one of the highest honours in the game. The club motto is 'Rugby football is a game for gentlemen in all classes, but never for a bad sportsman in any class.' Players don the black-and-white hooped jersey with pride, but each is allowed to wear his club socks as a further badge of honour and respect for the particular rugby community he represents. All Barbarians selections also include at least one player who has been uncapped at international level.

— FIELD GOALS —

Until 1905, when it was abolished, players were able to score four points for their side by kicking a field goal. This form of scoring could occur only in open play, with the ball having to be kicked soccer-style off the floor and over the crossbar.

— NOT SO CANNY SCOTS —

When the 1905 New Zealanders (Dave Gallaher's All Blacks 'Originals') arrived in Scotland, the tourists' management asked for expenses from the notoriously parsimonious Scottish Rugby Union. In fact, they requested £200. The Scots answered that this was far more than the expected gate takings, and said that instead they could have 'just' the total receipts as their guarantee. The New Zealanders turned up for the match at Inverleith to find the ground packed and a take of £1,200 (£150,000 in today's terms) awaiting them. The SRU were not amused.

— ROMANIA'S MEDAL —

The first Olympic medal won by Romania came in 1924, when their rugby team took the bronze at the Paris Games. Beaten by both France and gold-medal winners the United States, however, they achieved their historic medal simply by turning up. In fact, only those three countries entered the event, which was the last time rugby has featured in the Olympics.

— WORLD CUP SEVENS WINNERS —

1993 ....England
1997 ....Fiji
2001 ....New Zealand

— WERE THE ALL BLACKS POISONED? —

Laurie Mains, coach of the 1995 New Zealand team at that year's World Cup, remains convinced that his players were deliberately poisoned on the night before the final against hosts South Africa. The All Blacks had been made favourites in the week leading up to the game, which the Springboks eventually won 15–12 after extra time and a dour but exciting struggle. Mains, however, revealed after the game that almost his entire squad of players had suffered food poisoning on the eve of the match after eating at their hotel in Sandton, and that a good number of them had therefore gone into the game feeling less than their best.

The incident was dismissed by the South Africans as a mere accident, but Mains has fanned the flames of the conspiracy theorists. Some say it was the work of patriotic South Africans desperate for their team to win, some claim malice, and others talk of betting rings and those who stood to win huge amounts of money if underdogs South Africa pulled off the victory. We'll probably never know.

— MARATHON MAN —

Ronnie Swyer, a great Wasps captain of the 1920s and 1930s, played in 301 consecutive games for the club in England. After making his debut in 1920, he missed two matches in the 1922–3 season, but then – apart from sitting out the Easter tour of Antwerp and Cologne in 1924 – he was an ever-present until being put out of action with an injury in November 1934.

Swyer was an established and inspiring captain by the time Wasps went through the 1930/1 season unbeaten, and he later became president of the club from 1955 to 1958 and again in their centenary season of 1966–7. Moreover, he wasn't just remarkable for his longevity as a rugby player; he was aged 101 when he died in 1995.

— HERO COOCHIE —

During the 1993 British Lions tour, England international Gareth Chilcott – then in his last year as Bath's long-serving combative hooker – was hailed as a hero after almost certainly saving a man from drowning in a white-water rafting accident in New Zealand. Chilcott was in the country leading a group of rugby supporters, and the raft on which he was travelling struck a fallen tree trunk in a particularly violent stretch of water and overturned. The tourist, whose life jacket had been torn off in the collision and who also could not swim, was held afloat in the white water by Chilcott – who had grabbed an overhanging branch with his other hand – for 40 minutes until help arrived.

— WHAT TO WEAR —

Apart from regulation shirts, shorts, socks and boots, all rugby players may wear the following:

1   Supports made from elasticated and washable materials;

2   Shoulder pads made of soft and thin material, to cover the shoulder and collarbone only;

3   Ankle supports, shinguards, mouthguards;

4   Headgear made from soft and thin material.

Players must NOT wear any equipment or support that is likely to cause injury (eg buckles, clips, rings, zips or rigid materials).

— THE VARSITY MATCH —

The first Varsity match between the universities of Oxford and Cambridge was played in 1872. The inaugural match was staged at Oxford and the 1873 fixture was played at Cambridge. Since then the game has always been staged in London; before moving to Twickenham in 1921, it was played for seven years at Kennington Oval, seven years at Blackheath and then 29 times at the Queen's Club in Kensington between 1887 and 1920.

— CUP-FINAL ATTENDANCES —

The attendance for the first final of the English clubs' knockout cup (now the Powergen Cup) in 1972, between Gloucester and Moseley, was just 10,500. Indeed, the record remained a pitiful 11,500 until the seventh final – when Gloucester beat Leicester 6–3 in 1978 – attracted 24,000. However, the graph of Cup Final crowds has gone up steadily over the last two decades. And when 68,000 saw Bath take their eighth title in 1994, beating Leicester, it was then a world record for a club game.

— CLYDE RATHBONE —

'I don't want to be only a Springbok. I want to be a great Springbok.' This is what Clyde Rathbone said after leading South Africa to victory in the 2002 Under 21 World Cup. He now plays for Australia.

— THE ENGLISH PUMA —

William Barry Holmes played international rugby against France twice in 1949, for two different countries. In February of that year he played for England against France at Twickenham while a student at Cambridge University. Fast forwarding on to August, he then appeared as Argentina's full back in the first Test against the French in Buenos Aires, in the first international match that France had played on South American soil.

— DANIEL CARROLL —

Flying wing Daniel Carroll is the only man in history to have won two Olympic gold medals for rugby union. Carroll won his first with Australia at the 1908 Games and his second with the United States team at the 1920 Olympics. He is also the only player to have been capped at senior level by both countries, playing for the Wallabies against Wales in 1908 and then, coincidentally, against the United States in 1912. After serving in the First World War with the US Army, having moved to America following that 1912 Wallaby tour, he was capped by the USA in 1920.

— THE '99' CALL —

Perhaps the most notorious in rugby history, the '99 call' was devised by British Lions captain Willie John McBride, who decided that the only way that his team were to gain the psychological upper hand over their fearsome 1974 Springbok opponents was 'to get our retaliation in first'.

McBride, having toured South Africa twice before as a player, knew the Springbok mentality and knew what had to be done. On that tour, none of the Lions ever took a backward step, and whenever trouble flared up the '99 call' was made. This was the sign for every Lion to start brawling with his nearest opponent. That way, McBride reasoned, the referee couldn't send off everybody, and the Springboks would never be able to intimidate individual members of his side.

The brutal third Test at Port Elizabeth was a classic example of the effectiveness of the '99 call'. McBride led the immediate reaction to the call, wading forwards 20 yards into the very heart of the Springbok pack, swinging punches with his right and left hands as he went. JPR Williams, the full back, sprinted 30 yards to join in the general mayhem and the Lions' show of solidarity succeeded in putting the wind up the South Africans. McBride's team didn't lose once on their 22-match tour.

— IRISH TRAILBLAZERS —

Ireland were the first of the home unions to undertake a tour of Argentina. Des O'Brien captained a squad popularly known as 'the Shamrocks' on a nine-match visit in 1952 – a tour which coincided with the country being in mourning following the death of Eva Perón. It was to Ireland, in 1973, that Argentina subsequently made their own first foray to play one of the home union nations.

— GOLD AND BLUE —

American forward Alan Chester Valentine is the only man to have won both an Olympic Gold medal and a University Blue at rugby football. Valentine won three Oxford rugby Blues between 1923 and 1925 while on a Rhodes scholarship at the university and represented the United States when they won the rugby gold at the 1924 Paris Olympics. He was also a fine lacrosse player, and captained Oxford to victory over Cambridge in this other sport in 1925.

— OH BROTHER —

When Ireland met Australia in 1927 (their first meeting, incidentally), there were no fewer than three sets of brothers on the field at Lansdowne Road. The Stephensons and McVickers lined up on the Irish side and the Fords played for Australia.

— BEATEN WORLD CUP FINALISTS XV —

15	Serge Blanco (France, 1987)
14	Jeff Wilson (New Zealand, 1995)
13	Jeremy Guscott (England, 1991)
12	Philippe Sella (France, 1987)
11	Jonah Lomu (New Zealand, 1995)
10	Rob Andrew (England, 1991)
9	Pierre Berbizier (France, 1987)
1	Craig Dowd (New Zealand, 1995)
2	Raphael Ibanez (France, 1999)
3	Jean-Pierre Garuet (France, 1987)
4	Paul Ackford (England, 1991)
5	Wade Dooley (England, 1991)
6	Olivier Magne (France, 1999)
7	Josh Kronfeld (New Zealand, 1995)
8	Zinzan Brooke (New Zealand, 1995)

Replacements: Frank Bunce (New Zealand, 1995)
Andrew Mehrtens (New Zealand, 1995)
Fabien Galthie (France, 1999)
Olo Brown (New Zealand, 1995)
Brian Moore (England, 1991)
Fabien Pelous (France, 1999)
Peter Winterbottom (England, 1991)

— A SIGHT FOR SORE EYE —

On their 1974 tour, the British Lions came up against a player named Johann de Bruyn in one of their provincial matches. He only had one good eye, and before each game he used to remove his glass eye and fill up the hole with Vaseline. 'There was Vaseline dripping down his face out of this hole,' said Lions prop Mike Burton. 'It was a horrible sight, and you could hardly bear to look at him.'

— PREMIERSHIP RECORDS, 1997–2004 —

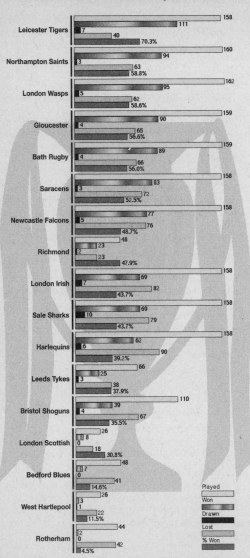

Leicester Tigers
158
111
7
40
70.3%

Northampton Saints
160
94
3
63
58.8%

London Wasps
162
95
5
62
58.6%

Gloucester
159
90
4
65
56.6%

Bath Rugby
159
89
4
66
56.0%

Saracens
158
83
3
72
52.5%

Newcastle Falcons
158
77
5
76
48.7%

Richmond
48
23
2
23
47.9%

London Irish
158
69
7
82
43.7%

Sale Sharks
158
69
10
79
43.7%

Harlequins
158
62
6
90
39.2%

Leeds Tykes
66
25
3
38
37.9%

Bristol Shoguns
110
39
4
67
35.5%

London Scottish
26
8
0
18
30.8%

Bedford Blues
48
7
0
41
14.6%

West Hartlepool
26
3
1
22
11.5%

Rotherham
44
2
0
42
4.5%

Played
Won
Drawn
Lost
% Won

— ALL BLACKS FAN'S ADVICE —

'Remember, it's a team game. Make sure everyone passes to Jonah.'
*– Message faxed to New Zealand captain Sean Fitzpatrick
on the eve of the 1995 World Cup final against
South Africa in Johannesburg. The All Blacks lost.*

— IAN McGEECHAN —

It's difficult to look beyond Ian McGeechan in the elite list of those who have contributed the most, both on and off the field, to the proud history of the British Lions. As a Scotland centre, McGeechan toured South Africa in 1974 and New Zealand in 1977. He then coached the 1989 Lions to victory in Australia, and although his 1993 team lost 2–1 in New Zealand, he bounced back by leading the 1997 tourists to an epic 2–1 win in South Africa. In 2005, he is going back to New Zealand as one of Sir Clive Woodward's four assistant coaches.

— THE NOT-SO-GENTLE PUT-DOWN —

Bath's England prop Victor Ubogu once asked Jack Rowell, who coached him at both club and international level, why he had taken an instant dislike to him. Quick as a flash, Rowell replied, 'Because it saved time, Victor.'

— HARRY READ —

When Ireland scrum-half Harry Read reported that he was feeling unwell on the morning of the 1912 international against Wales at Balmoral, Belfast, he was nevertheless persuaded to play and, by all accounts, had an outstanding match as the Irish triumphed 12–5. That evening, though, he was still complaining of feeling ill and so was taken to hospital for a check-up. It was then discovered that he had played a full international despite suffering from measles.

— TEN-TRY MAN —

On 11 October 1994, Hong Kong full back Ashley Billington set a record for international try-scoring that might take some beating. As Hong Kong trounced Singapore 164–13 in a World Cup qualifier, Billington crossed for a remarkable ten tries.

— BIRTH OF THE FIRST WORLD CUP —

In 1987, Australia and New Zealand were the architects of the inaugural Rugby World Cup. Scotland and Ireland voted against it in the historic Paris meeting of March 1985, when it was finally decided to go ahead with the tournament. The six IRFB nations in favour were Australia, New Zealand, South Africa, England, Wales and France. However, the agreement was to stage it for one experimental tournament only.

— LOVE CONQUERS ALL —

Players suffering from homesickness, and absence from an especially close friend, are nothing new on Lions tours. In 1955, when the British Lions were in South Africa, key fly-half Cliff Morgan became so down at the lack of letters from his girlfriend back home that his form began to slip badly. So, too, did that of the team, so influential a player was Morgan.

Nothing had been heard for weeks from the young lady in question, until the players reached Cape Town. The next morning, the 'duty boy' – a player whose tasks for the day included collecting the mail – walked into the team room at breakfast and called for silence. 'Gentlemen, I have important news,' he said, in a stern voice. Everyone looked up as he revealed from behind his back a sheaf of letters and said simply, 'These – all of these – letters have arrived for one player: Cliff Morgan.'

Wild cheers greeted the news as the letters were hurled into the air. Morgan's face broke into a smile not seen for days and, soon afterwards, his and the team's best form re-emerged.

— THE BIRTH OF CANADIAN RUGBY —

Rugby was introduced into Canada in the 1880s by an Englishman named A St G Hammersley, who had played against Scotland in England's 1871 Calcutta Cup match.

— FIRST COLOURED SPRINGBOK —

Hugely gifted Western Province centre Errol Tobias became the first coloured player to pull on a Springbok jersey when he was selected for South Africa's tour of South America in 1980.

— A ROUND DOZEN – TWICE! —

Desmond Connor played 12 times for Australia and then 12 times for New Zealand in the late 1950s and early 1960s. After switching allegiances, he never appeared on the losing side for the All Blacks, and seven of those 12 wins were against Australia.

— BROTHERS A WORLD APART —

Bernie and Sean McCahill both played international rugby as centres during the 1990s, but Bernie played for New Zealand and his brother Sean for Ireland.

— THE ARMS PARK —

Cardiff Arms Park, the famous rugby amphitheatre now superseded on the same site by the Millennium Stadium, was so called because it was built on playing fields that took their name from the Cardiff Arms Inn, which at the end of the 19th century stood next to the Angel Hotel opposite the ground.

— TWO COUNTRIES, ONE WORLD CUP —

Great French forward of the 1990s Abdel Benazzi represented his native Morocco (against Belgium) in a zonal qualifying match for the 1991 World Cup before switching to the French national team and playing for them in the tournament itself later that year.

— A 70-YEAR-OLD TUNE —

When officiating the Australia v South Africa game during the 1995 World Cup, referee Derek Bevan used the same whistle that his Welsh compatriot Albert Freethy had used when refereeing the England v New Zealand international in 1925.

— VC AND DSO —

Tom Crean, who played for Ireland in the 1890s, won the Victoria Cross during the Boer War and then the Distinguished Service Order during the First World War.

— SHORT NAMES XV —

Here is an international rugby XV entirely made up of players with a surname only three letters long:

15	Bruce Hay (Scotland)
14	Jean-Pierre Lux (France)
13	Chris Rea (Scotland)
12	John Dee (England)
11	Chris Oti (England)
10	Grant Fox (New Zealand)
9	Phil Cox (Australia)
1	Phil Orr (Ireland)
2	Yannick Bru (France)
3	Richard Loe (New Zealand)
4	Phil May (Wales)
5	Ben Kay (England)
6	Andy Dun (England)
7	Andre Vos (South Africa)
8	Pat Lam (Samoa)

— HORTON'S RECORD —

Nigel Horton, Moseley's giant lock who was infamous for being sent off in the first ever final of the English clubs' knockout cup in 1972, is the only Englishman to have played international rugby in the 1960s, 1970s and 1980s.

— THE BOOTS —

Studs on boots must be a maximum of 18mm in length. Old-fashioned boots were large and heavy leather items, coming up well above the ankle so as to protect it. Modern boots tend to be cut more in the soccer style, as this assists with speed over the ground.

— RUGBY'S REAL WILSON OF THE WIZARD? —

Sporting history is dotted with great all-rounders, from the far-off days of Englishman CB Fry, through those of players such as Eric Liddell and Denis Compton, to the modern achievements of the likes of Jeff Wilson. But what about Irish doctor Kevin O'Flanagan?

In successive weeks, in 1946, Flanagan played rugby for Ireland against France at Lansdowne Road and then soccer for Northern Ireland against Scotland in Belfast. He would have played another rugby international against England seven days later, too, but for being held up by bad weather as he attempted to fly over from his London-based medical practice on the Saturday of the game. An amateur, and a winger in both footballing codes, he played his club soccer mainly for Arsenal and his rugby for London Irish.

What's more, Flanagan was a two-handicap golfer who was once denied the Irish Amateur Championship by the legendary Joe Carr, and was also Irish sprint and long-jump champion. He would have competed at the Olympics but for the Second World War, although he later became medical officer for the Ireland Olympic team at four Games and was elected to the International Olympic Committee in 1976.

— FROM BALL BOYS TO GRAND SLAM HEROES —

The epic 1971 match between Scotland and Wales at Murrayfield has long been hailed as one of the greatest in International Championship history. Six tries were scored, the lead changed hands four times, and in the end it was John Taylor's dramatic touchline conversion of Gerald Davies' last-minute try ('the greatest conversion since St Paul's') that gave Wales a 19–18 win and kept them on track for an eventual Grand Slam victory. Two 13-year-old ball boys sat entranced that afternoon by the heroics they witnessed in front of them – and both Jim and Finlay Calder went on to play leading roles in Scotland's Grand Slams of 1984 and 1990 respectively.

— APPROPRIATE NAMES —

Two rugby players have represented the country of their surnames: Ken Scotland (1957) and John Ireland (1876).

— PAT HARROWER —

London Scottish full back Pat Harrower had an odd claim to fame. In his sole rugby international, he helped Scotland to a 0–0 draw against Wales at Hamilton Crescent, Glasgow, in 1885, one of only two such results between the two countries. Then, 20 years later, in 1905, he refereed the FA Cup soccer final in which Aston Villa beat Newcastle United 2–0 at Crystal Palace.

— TOO YOUNG —

Kenneth MacLeod was just a 15-year old schoolboy centre at Fettes College when, in 1903, the Scotland selectors asked headmaster Dr Heard for permission to pick him for the forthcoming international against Wales. Dr Heard refused on the grounds that the boy was too young.

Two years later, in February 1905, the Scottish selectors actually went ahead and named him in their side to play the Welsh. Again, Dr Heard refused permission – this time on the grounds he had not been consulted! Eventually, after starting his studies at Cambridge University later that year, MacLeod finally made his Scotland debut against the touring New Zealanders on 18 November 1905. He was 17 years and 9 months old, and went on to win ten caps before retiring from international rugby before he had reached 21.

— SOSPAN FACH —

Mae bys Meri Ann wedi brifo
A Dafydd y gwas ddim, yn iach.
Mae'r baban yn y crud yn crio
A'r gath wedi scramo Johnny bach.

(Chorus)
Sospan fach yn berwi ar y tan
Sospan fawr yn berwi ar y llawr,
A'r gath wedi scramo Johnny bach

Dai bach y sowldiwr
Dai bach y sowldiwr
Dai bach y sowldiwr
A'i gwt I grys e mas

★

Sospan fach yn berwi ar y tan
Sospan fawr yn berwi ar y llawr,
A'r gath wedi scramo Johnny bach.

— THE SUN NEVER SHINES... —

In 1977, the Lions had to put up with a difficult tour of New Zealand, in terms of the weather, which was terrible wherever they went. The rugby grounds became awash with mud and water, it was cold, the sun was rarely sighted and the players lost three of the four Test matches.

Some blamed the fact that there was too strong a Welsh influence on the trip. Of the 33 players the Lions used on the tour, no fewer than 15 came from Wales. Furthermore, the Lions that year were captained by a Welshman, Phil Bennett of Llanelli, and coached by another, John Dawes, who had been captain of the 1971 Lions in New Zealand. Long afterwards, Bennett admitted, 'I should never have accepted the captaincy.'

By contrast, there were only six Englishmen, five Scots (four of them backs) and four Irishmen (three of them in the forwards). Morale was never that high, and the management seemed paranoid about any criticism or comparison with past Lions tours, yet the Lions won all their opening eight provincial matches. In fact, of their 21 provincial games, they lost only one, to New Zealand Universities.

When it came to the Test series, however, it was another story, and the harsh fact was that those particular Lions threw away that Test series. Their forward power was so overwhelming that it should have settled the series and guaranteed the Lions' victory in the Tests. As it turned out, their backs were so inept that, despite having the lion's share of possession, they simply frittered away the quality balls delivered to them. The All Blacks somehow managed to snatch the final Test 10–9 in Auckland, after an horrific defensive mix-up by the Lions, so that all the hard work and total superiority of the Lions forwards went to waste. Men like Fran Cotton and Peter Wheeler – the Englishmen in the Lions' front row – were rendered speechless by the outcome.

— GREAT TRIES 3 —

JEAN-LUC SADOURNY
FRANCE v NEW ZEALAND
AUCKLAND, 1994

This is a score that will forever be known as 'the try from the end of the world', following a comment afterwards from Philippe Saint-Andre, the France captain and the man who started the length-of-the-field move that earned the most dramatic of 23–20 victories. Saint-Andre actually said, 'It was a counter-attack from the end of the world – a true image of French rugby,' but the central sound-bite image stuck, and he was also right to say that it summed up all that was good about Gallic flair.

1 On 3 July 1994, France were losing the second Test at Auckland by 20–16 when the game entered injury time. The massed Eden Park stands were in a frenzy. New Zealand had lost the opening Test to the French by a humiliating 22–8 in Christchurch, and the All Blacks had reacted furiously with a huge forward effort. As the clock ticked down, it looked as if Kiwi revenge was going to be sweet. Then, however, fly-half Stephen Bachop kicked long to the right side of the field in a bid to find touch by the corner flag, but the ball bounced in-field and was picked up 10m inside his own 22 by Saint-Andre.

2 Saint-Andre had no intention of touching the ball down for a drop-out. He knew time was running out and that he must try to launch one last counter-attack. From in front of his own posts he set off on a weaving run that took him past three onrushing New Zealanders, before linking with hooker Jean-Marc Gonzalez.

3 Gonzalez made a little ground, but was then tackled by Mark Cooksley, the All Blacks' lock. France, however, quickly won the ruck and the ball was fed out by Christophe Deylaud, the fly-half, to Abdel Benazzi, who charged upfield.

4 Right wing Emile N'tamack was up in support to take over from Benazzi and inject real pace into the attack. N'tamack surged over the halfway line.

5 It was flanker Laurent Cabannes, however, who changed the angle of the attack when he latched onto a pass from N'tamack. Cabannes'

contribution opened up a crucial gap in the remaining, scrambling All Blacks defence and allowed Yann Delaigue to keep the move alive.

6   Delaigue then found scrum-half Guy Accoceberry, who at first put his head down in an attempted sprint for the line. Realising that he might be caught, however, he had the good sense to ship the ball on to the quicker Sadourny, who had the privilege of going over for the greatest try seen at Eden Park. The ball had passed through nine pairs of hands. The French were jubilant, and the whole of New Zealand was stunned.

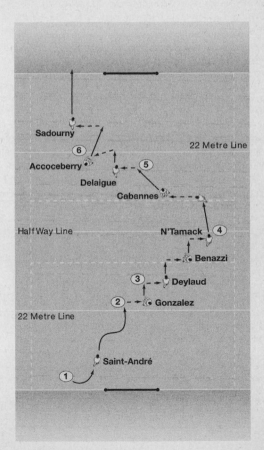

— AIR TRAVEL —

These days rugby teams jet around the globe in matter-of-fact fashion, but the first international side to travel by air to a rugby-playing destination were the 1947 All Blacks. They travelled by flying boat from Auckland to Australia, with their squad split into two separate batches for trips made on successive days.

— NO STONE UNTURNED —

In the run-up to the 2003 World Cup, Sir Clive Woodward was passionate about doing everything he and his support team could possibly do to give the England team an edge over their opponents during the tournament. This attention to detail even included using an anti-bugging device to make sure that team-room meetings weren't the subject of any listening-in by the opposition.

Woodward, predictably, was mocked for being paranoid in much of the media – especially in Australia, of course – but he made no apologies for admitting that his staff had regularly swept hotel, team and changing rooms for electronic listening devices. He said, 'We have a machine that anyone can buy in the shops that checks for bugs. We have this little device – and it's no bigger than a matchbox – and Tony Biscombe, who is our IT man, goes round the players' hotel rooms and the team rooms and makes sure there are no devices. Sometimes people don't understand the huge stakes that we're playing for, and we don't want to take any chances – and we don't. It's just common sense. We've done it for a couple of years now, and it's our standard way of operating. It's just security, and we take security very seriously.'

Woodward brought in the policy as a result of his belief that the 2001 British Lions were the victims of some spying on their losing tour of Australia. 'The Aussies purported to know all the Lions' line-out calls,' he pointed out.

— STEVE MCDOWELL —

New Zealand prop Steve McDowell was selected to represent his country at judo in the 1980 Moscow Olympics. Unfortunately, the Kiwis then joined the multi-nation boycott of the Games, and McDowell's hopes of an Olympic medal were dashed.

— THE FLAGS —

The recommended height of flag sticks employed on a rugby field is 1.2m (4ft). Flags should be placed at the four corners of the main playing area, and also at the four corners of the in-goal areas. Additonally, flags should be placed at points outside the touchline but adjacent to the halfway line and both 22m lines. There should, therefore, be 14 flags used in the correct marking-up of a rugby field: seven on each side.

— ENGLAND'S WORLD CUP CAPTAINS —

Only three men have captained England at the World Cup: Mike Harrison (Wakefield) in 1987, Will Carling (Harlequins) in 1991 and 1995, and Martin Johnson (Leicester) in 1999 and 2003.

— BARBARIANS FROM THE STEPPES? —

A small piece of rugby history was made during the Barbarians' Easter tour of Wales in 1990, during which two Russians – Igor Mironov and Alexander Tikhonov – became the first players from their country to represent the famous club.

— GOAL FROM A MARK —

Dropping a goal from a mark was a method of scoring which was abandoned in 1977/8. In 1903, playing for New Zealand against Australia, Billy Wallace achieved the unique feat of dropping two goals from marks.

— FIRST TRY AT TWICKENHAM —

Frederick Chapman of Hartlepool Rovers scored the first international try at Twickenham, during England's 11–6 victory against Wales on 15 January 1910. This was the first international match to be played on what is still affectionately called 'Billy Williams' old cabbage patch', in honour of the RFU committee man and former referee who led the search for a site on which to build a permanent headquarters for English rugby.

— BRITISH LIONS FULL TEST RECORD —

Year	Country	P	W	D	L	F	A
1891	South Africa	3	3	0	0	11	0
1896	South Africa	4	3	0	1	34	16
1899	Australia	4	3	0	1	38	23
1903	South Africa	3	0	2	1	10	18
1904	Australia &	3	3	0	0	50	3
	New Zealand	1	0	0	1	3	9
1908	New Zealand	3	0	1	2	8	64
1910	South Africa	3	1	0	2	23	38
1924	South Africa	4	0	1	3	15	43
1930	New Zealand &	4	1	0	3	34	53
	Australia	1	0	0	1	5	6
1938	South Africa	3	1	0	2	36	61
1950	New Zealand &	4	0	1	3	20	34
	Australia	2	2	0	0	43	9
1955	South Africa	4	2	0	2	49	75
1959	Australia &	2	2	0	0	41	9
	New Zealand	4	1	0	3	42	57
1962	South Africa	4	0	1	3	20	48
1966	Australia &	2	2	0	0	42	8
	New Zealand	4	0	0	4	32	79
1968	South Africa	4	0	1	3	38	61
1971	New Zealand	4	2	1	1	48	42
1974	South Africa	4	3	1	0	79	34
1977	New Zealand	4	1	0	3	41	54
1980	South Africa	4	1	0	3	68	77
1983	New Zealand	4	0	0	4	26	78
1989	Australia	3	2	0	1	50	60
1993	New Zealand	3	1	0	2	51	57
1997	South Africa	3	2	0	1	60	66
2001	Australia	3	1	0	2	66	77

— LONG WAIT FOR WRONG SLAM —

England didn't lose all four matches of a Five Nations Championship season until 1976.

— A TOUCH TOO LATE —

The 1974 British Lions had a thoroughly controversial ending to their unbeaten tour of South Africa. During the final Test, in Johannesburg, right at the end of the match and with the scores level at 13–13, Irish flanker Fergus Slattery crossed the Springbok line in the last minute.

The South African referee, Max Baise, admitted that the Irishman had touched the ball down, but claimed that he'd just blown the final whistle for the end of the game, seconds earlier, although none of the Lions had heard it. It robbed the Lions of a 100 per cent record and a 4–0 Test whitewash of the Springboks. As it was, they finished with 21 wins from 22 games and one draw. But, as one local said later, 'That decision showed that the ref had some brains in his head. He has to stay in this country after the Lions have gone home.'

— BILL BEAUMONT —

'Beaumont habitually wore the forlorn expression of a man who has just inferred, from the cold, creeping sensation in his socks, that the dog has been sick in his shoes.'

– *Giles Smith in* The Times, *November 2004*

— HISTORY OF THE HAKA —

The word 'Haka' refers to a Maori dance, and that performed by the All Blacks prior to every match derives from a celebratory song which is believed to have been composed in the 1820s by Chief Te Rauparaha, of the Ngati Toa tribe, after his life had been saved by the wife of a neighbouring chief. The mention of a 'hairy man' in the song is a reference to this chief, from whom Te Rauparaha hid by crawling under the skirts of his wife.

— WELSH CAPTAIN FROM DOWN UNDER —

James Bevan, the very first Wales rugby captain, was actually born in Brisbane, Australia, having come to Britain as a child and attending Hereford Cathedral School. Bevan led Wales against England at Blackheath in 1881.

— THE GREATEST LIONS XV EVER? —

Comparisons of players from different eras is of endless fascination to sports lovers everywhere. What about this for an all-time Lions XV, drawn from only those players who have represented the British Isles since the Second World War?

15	JPR Williams (Wales)
14	Gerald Davies (Wales)
13	Jeremy Guscott (England)
12	Brian O'Driscoll (Ireland)
11	Tony O'Reilly (Ireland)
10	Barry John (Wales)
9	Gareth Edwards (Wales)
1	Fran Cotton (England)
2	John Pullin (England)
3	Graham Price (Wales)
4	Willie John McBride (Ireland, captain)
5	Martin Johnson (England)
6	Lawrence Dallaglio (England)
7	Fergus Slattery (Ireland)
8	Mervyn Davies (Wales)

Replacements: Andy Irvine (Scotland)
Mike Gibson (Ireland)
Terry Holmes (Wales)
Ian McLauchlan (Scotland)
Peter Wheeler (England)
Gordon Brown (Scotland)
Richard Hill (England)

— THE ONLY JUAN —

United States Eagles centre Juan Grobler was the unlikely scorer of the only try conceded in the tournament by 1999 World Cup winners Australia. Grobler's score came in the USA's 55–19 defeat against the Wallabies at Limerick.

— SHORTEST CAREERS —

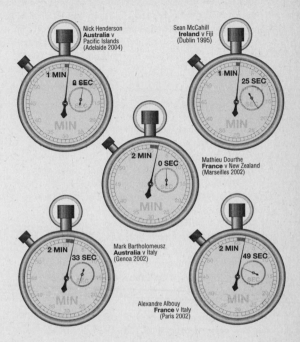

Nick Henderson
Australia v
Pacific Islands
(Adelaide 2004)

1 MIN 0 SEC

Sean McCahill
Ireland v Fiji
(Dublin 1995)

1 MIN 25 SEC

Mathieu Dourthe
France v New Zealand
(Marseilles 2002)

2 MIN 0 SEC

Mark Bartholomeusz
Australia v Italy
(Genoa 2002)

2 MIN 33 SEC

Alexandre Albouy
France v Italy
(Paris 2002)

2 MIN 49 SEC

— HOUSE OF PAIN —

This evocative nickname was given to Dunedin's Carisbrook Stadium, perhaps New Zealand rugby's most distinctive and atmospheric venue. The ground was leased from the Presbyterian Church for almost a century before the Otago Rugby Union bought the freehold in 1981, their centenary year. It was first called the 'House of Pain' in the 1990s, when Brent Pope, the Otago number eight, referred to it thus when talking about a ferocious training session organised for the provincial team by Laurie Mains, who also coached the All Blacks from 1992 to 1995. The soubriquet was seized on by rugby fans, because it seemed an apt description of an arena that's never anything less than intimidating for any visiting side, provincial or international.

— THE UNKINDEST CUT? —

Wayne 'Buck' Shelford suffered one of the most eye-watering injuries in rugby history when the All Blacks were downed 16-3 by France in 1986 in what the New Zealand number eight called 'the hardest match I have ever played in'. The All Blacks were stunned by the sustained savagery of the French forward play, and Shelford needed 22 stitches after the game to the damage he had sustained to his scrotum.

— THE IRISH DOUBLE ACT —

Two of the greatest players, in terms of vivacity and wit, that the British Lions ever selected came together on the 1959 tour of New Zealand. Tony O'Reilly was a pre-tour selection, but his fellow Irishman and great friend AA (Andy) Mulligan was called to New Zealand when the Scottish scrum-half Stan Coughtrie was injured and had to return home. On the trip, Mulligan and O'Reilly struck up their friendship that endured until the former's death in 2000. They entertained the team hugely on long bus trips, and even took over the aircraft intercom on several flights, doing impressions of the tour management, fellow players and others whom they had encountered.

When the team got to Auckland Airport to await the flight home at the end of the tour, Mulligan invaded the airport's intercom office and broadcast bogus directions for non-existent flights and the like, to the general amusement of all. As one Lion said years later, 'I suspect many of those flights he redirected are still up in the sky, awaiting instructions to land.'

New Zealand had neither seen nor heard anything like them. Indeed, the duo were considered so good on air, and so professional, that they were invited to host their own show on a popular New Zealand radio station during the tour. The Lions tour management thought that this might be taking things too far, but the merriment and chaos created by the two Irishmen helped to make the whole tour go with a real swing.

— HONOURS LIST —

In the aftermath of England's 2003 World Cup win, the whole squad was honoured in the 2004 New Year's honours list, as were various others associated with the victory. The whole list is as follows:

- **KNIGHTS BATCHELOR:** Clive Woodward OBE

- **CBE:** Martin Johnson OBE

- **OBE:** Francis Baron, Jason Leonard MBE, Andy Robinson, Jonny Wilkinson MBE

- **MBE:** Stuart Abbott, Dave Alred, Neil Back, Iain Balshaw, Kyran Bracken, Mike Catt, Ben Cohen, Martin Corry, Lawrence Dallaglio, Matt Dawson, Andy Gomarsall, Paul Grayson, Will Greenwood, Danny Grewcock, Richard Hill, Ben Kay, Phil Larder, Josh Lewsey, Dan Luger, Lewis Moody, Dave Reddin, Mark Regan, Jason Robinson, Simon Shaw, Steve Thompson, Mike Tindall, Phil Vickery, Dorian West, Julian White, Trevor Woodman, Joe Worsley.

— EALES AND HORAN —

John Eales and Tim Horan, of Australia, are the only two men to have started two World Cup finals and emerge as winners on both occasions. They did so in 1991 and 1999, with the personable, spring-heeled line-out specialist lock forward and occasional goal-kicker Eales – nicknamed 'Nobody', as in 'Nobody's perfect' – also captaining the Wallabies to their 1999 success against France.

— TALLEST POSTS —

The tallest rugby goalposts in the world are at Wednesbury, in England. They stand 38.1m (125ft) high and are made of tubular steel. Each post is set in almost 4.5m³ of concrete. In contrast, the posts at Twickenham stand just 12.8m (42ft) high, while those at the Millennium Stadium in Cardiff are 16.8m (55ft) in height.

THE LIFE AND TIMES OF SIR CLIVE WOODWARD
— (SO FAR) —

1956 Born on 6 January in Ely, Cambridgeshire, the son of an RAF pilot.

1980 Makes England debut against Ireland and plays throughout the Grand Slam, winning the campaign under Bill Beaumont. Selected for that summer's British Lions tour of South Africa, playing in two Tests.

1981 Completes a hat-trick of English Cup final wins with his club, Leicester.

1983 Tours New Zealand with the Lions, but doesn't play in the Test side.

1984 Makes the last of his 21 appearances for England, against Wales, after scoring four tries in his England career.

1985 Emigrates for business reasons to Australia, where he plays club rugby for Manly.

1990 Returns to England and begins a coaching stint at Henley, a Southwest Division Two side.

1994 Joins London Irish as coach, having taken Henley to the verge of national league status.

1997 Joins Bath for a short spell as head coach, having also by then been in charge of England Under 21s.

1997 Succeeds Jack Rowell as England's first professional head coach, at a time when the team are ranked sixth in the world.

1998 Takes severely depleted England squad on infamous 'Tour to Hell' in Australia, where they lose 76–0 at Brisbane, before going on to similar defeat in New Zealand and South Africa.

1999 England fall at quarter-final stage of the World Cup, losing to South Africa.

1999– bb 2001 England lose three successive Grand Slam matches: to Wales in 1999, to Scotland in 2000 and to Ireland in 2001.

2002 Awarded OBE by the Queen.

2003 England win first Grand Slam under Woodward, beating Ireland 42–6 in glorious fashion in Dublin to clinch it.

2003 Summer tour brings victories over New Zealand in Wellington and Australia in Melbourne. England are demonstrably ready for the World Cup, despite the longest-winning run in their history (14 matches) ending when a second-string side is beaten narrowly by France in Marseilles in a penultimate World Cup warm-up match. England are ranked number one in the world for the first time.

2003 World Cup is won in Sydney, with Australia being beaten 20–17 in extra time.

2004 England lose at home to Ireland and away to France in Six Nations Championship and then, on a summer tour, lose twice in New Zealand and once in Australia.

2004 Woodward resigns on 2 September, and his resignation is accepted with immediate effect by RFU. He says his work with England would have clashed with his job as head coach to the 2005 British Lions tour of New Zealand. He also indicates that, following the Lions tour, he would like to involve himself in soccer.

— THE GOAL POSTS —

The goal posts on the rugby pitch, and the padding surrounding them, are part of the goal-line, which is part of in-goal. If an attacking player is first to ground the ball against the post or the padding, a try is scored.

— RUGBY CLUB THIEF —

Fifty-two-year-old Alan Phillips from Cambridge was jailed for three and a half years in 2004 after pleading guilty to charges of theft from more than 50 rugby clubs the length and breadth of England. Phillips admitted to posing as a club official and walking away with valuables totalling an estimated £45,000. Initially, he admitted to thefts at rugby clubs at Wellington, Glastonbury, Shrewsbury, Winchester, Newbury, Esher and four in Cumbria, but then went on to confess to another 40 or more.

— THE BREAKAWAY CLUBS —

The following clubs were the founder members of the Northern Rugby Football Union – the forerunner of Rugby League – in 1895:

Batley
Bradford
Brighouse Rangers
Broughton Rangers
Halifax
Huddersfield
Hull
Hunslet
Leeds
Leigh
Liversedge
Manningham
Oldham
Rochdale Hornets
St Helens
Tyldesley
Wakefield Trinity
Warrington
Widnes
Wigan

Dewsbury also attended the historic meeting on 29 August 1985 at the George Hotel in Huddersfield, but they were the only club initially to refuse to resign Rugby Football Union membership. Stockport and Runcorn joined up soon after the meeting, to make the first Northern Rugby Football Union a competition involving 22 clubs.

Eight more northern clubs joined in 1896 – including Swinton, Salford, Castleford and Bramley – and for the first two years of its existence the Northern Rugby Union matches were played to the same laws as amateur rugby union.

The term 'rugby league' was coined in Australia in 1907, and wasn't officially adopted in England until 1922. Then the Northern Rugby Union renamed itself the Rugby Football League.

— TEN FAMOUS PLAYER NICKNAMES —

The Claw – Peter Clohessy
Uncle Fester – Keith Wood
Le Petit Général – Pierre Berbizier
God – Brian O'Driscoll
Nobody – John Eales (as in 'Nobody's Perfect')
The Abbot – Hugh McLeod
Pine Tree – Colin Meads
Mighty Mouse – Ian McLauchlan
The Bear – Iain Milne
The Bayonne Express – Patrice Lagisquet

— TOM VOYCES —

London Wasps and England wing Tom Voyce is named after his great uncle, Gloucester's Thomas Anthony Voyce, who won 27 caps for England and two for the British Lions in the 1920s. Uncle Tom was a tearaway flanker who, together with inspirational captain Wavell Wakefield, prop Ronald Cove-Smith and fellow back-rower Arthur Blakiston, made the England pack of that era the best in the world. In all, three Grand Slams were won by England in four years in the early 1920s. Tom Voyce, Sr, remained involved in rugby after his playing days had ended and became president of both Gloucesteshire's club and the RFU.

— NORRIS McWHIRTER —

Best known as the man who, with twin brother Ross, founded the Guinness Book of Records – which has become the second biggest selling work of non-fiction after the Bible – Norris McWhirter was also a former prolific try-scorer for Saracens. Born in Southgate in 1925, he was also one of the official time-keepers at Sir Roger Bannister's first sub-four-minute mile at Oxford in May 1954 and had the distinction of reading out the result of the race to a hushed, and then jubilant, crowd. He represented Scotland and Great Britain as a sprinter and made his Saracens debut in the 1947/8 season. He was a lifelong supporter of the club until his death, on 19 April 2004.

— WORLD CUP WINDFALL —

Victory in the 2003 World Cup has made English rugby considerably richer. According to the RFU's accounts for the 2003/4 financial year, the sport's cash balances rose by more than 61 per cent from £20.7 million to £33.4 million, even after a sum of £14.5 million had been distributed among clubs and county associations (constituent bodies). The turnover generated by Twickenham's Rugby Store increased from £4 million in 2003 to £7.7 million in 2004.

— CHAUFFEUR-DRIVEN SWAN SONG —

In 1970, Tony O'Reilly – even by then considered mainly as a legendary former Lions wing of the 1950s – hadn't played international rugby for seven years when he received one of the most bizarre call-ups that top-class sport has witnessed. It also enabled Twickenham to chuckle at one of the best lines ever shouted out from a watching spectator.

O'Reilly, then 33 and playing for London Irish purely for fun, was already a senior and successful businessman in his role of heading up the London office of HJ Heinz. The astonishing comeback story began on a Thursday evening, in a central London nightclub, where O'Reilly was busily entertaining some corporate clients at a function. Suddenly, a telegram arrived for him, and on reading the missive O'Reilly had the shock of his life. The Ireland selectors were requesting him to report for squad training at the HAC Club, in the City of London, at 10am the following morning. It transpired that Bill Brown, the first-choice Irish right wing, had been injured that day in training and Ireland needed an emergency stand-by replacement.

The next morning, a chauffeur-driven Rolls-Royce purred through the gates of the HAC Club and, at a few minutes to ten, out stepped O'Reilly with boots in hand and in full view of the rest of the waiting Ireland squad. A huge cheer went up from the players, and the story of O'Reilly's grand entrance onto the training ground had made the newspapers, of course, by the time the day of the match dawned. O'Reilly was by now confirmed as a starter, despite being clearly less than international-match fit and more than a touch thicker around the waistband than he had been in his glory days. He got through the game though – his 29th, and definitely his final cap – despite taking a knock early on when he was tested by a high ball and, all too predictably, flattened beneath an England pack that had charged up *en masse* in their relish to take a chunk or two out of the great man. As

O'Reilly staggered, eventually, to his feet after the clattering, a strange and sudden hush descended on the baying Twickenham stands. And, out of the momentary stillness, an Irish voice piped up, 'And you can kick his fucking chaffeur, too!'

Even O'Reilly, it is said, laughed out loud as spectators and players from both sides fell about.

— JAPAN'S WORLD CUP BID —

A bid to take the World Cup outside rugby's traditional strongholds was made by Japan in late 2004. New Zealand and South Africa are also in the race to host the 2011 event, which will follow the French tournament in 2007, but the Japanese believe that the time will be right by then to open up the World Cup to the potentially huge new audiences of the Far East. 'Until now, the World Cup has been held in countries from the Six Nations or Tri-Nations,' said Japan Rugby Football Union secretary Koji Tokumasu. 'We think that it is time for rugby to go global. Japan is ready to host the tournament, and we are looking forward to welcoming the world of rugby to Japan.'

— ICE BATHS —

The old heroes of rugby didn't take them, of course, on their way to the after-match bonhomie at the bar, but there are good scientific reasons why the modern-day player is immersed regularly in ice baths. Each training session and every match is followed by an ice bath at most of the top clubs these days, and although this is obviously not a favourite part of the modern routine, it is something that the players appreciate as beneficial. The idea is to lower yourself into the ice-cold water for a certain period of time. The icy water constricts the blood vessels, and so, when the players get out of the bath and step into a warm shower, they quickly feel a glow as their blood vessels enlarge back to normal and the blood flows more quickly. This process is usually repeated several times, as the constriction and expansion of the vessels has a flushing effect on the lactic acid that has built up in the muscles. This, in turn, reduces significantly the soreness or stiffness a player feels after the strenuous effort of a match or tough training session.

— A SONG FOR JONNY —

Andrew Motion, Britain's Poet Laureate, penned the following tribute to England's 2003 World Cup-winning team. It's called 'A Song For Jonny':

> Jonny, the power of your boot
> And the accurate heart-stopping route
> Of your goal as it ghosts
> Through Australian posts
> Is a triumph we gladly salute.
>
> Martin, the height of your leap
> And the gritty possession you keep
> Of the slippery ball
> In the ruck and the maul
> Is enough to make patriots weep.
>
> Jason, the speed of your feet
> And their side-stepping
> Hop-scotching beat
> As you touch down and score
> While the terraces roar
> Is the thing that makes chariots sweet.
>
> Forwards and backs, you have all
> Shown us wonderful ways to walk tall
> And together with Clive
> You will help us survive
> Our losses with other-shaped balls.

— THE SUPPORT STAFF —

The British Lions didn't take a properly recognised coach on any tour until as late as 1966, when Englishman JD Robins was given the job for the long trip to Australia and New Zealand. Before that, the Lions had always managed as best they could when it came to training. Traditionally, they had a manager and assistant manager, the latter handling much of the paperwork that accrued during the course of the tour. For example, in 1955, England centre Jeff Butterfield, who was a PE student at Loughborough, was deputed to organise some of the training sessions on that Lions tour of South Africa, while on the 1959 tour of New Zealand the Lions captain, Ronnie Dawson, was given the unofficial task of organising his men's preparations for the matches on tour.

Contrast all that with the small army of coaching and back-up technical and medical staff selected to accompany the 2005 British Lions on their 11-match tour of New Zealand. The full list is worth noting, and is as follows:

Tour Manager: *Bill Beaumont*

Head Coach: *Sir Clive Woodward*

Assistant Coach: *Eddie O'Sullivan*

Assistant Coach: *Andy Robinson*

Assistant Coach: *Ian McGeechan*

Assistant Coach: *Gareth Jenkins*

Defence Coach: *Phil Larder*

Defence Coach: *Mike Ford*

Kicking Coach: *Dave Aldred*

Fitness Coach: *Dave Reddin*

Fitness Coach: *Craig White*

Video Analyst: *Tony Biscombe*

Video Analyst: *Gavin Scott*

Chief Executive: *John Feehan*

Team Manager: *Louise Ramsay*

Tour Doctor: *James Robson*

Doctor: *Gary O'Driscoll*

Physiotherapist: *Phil Pask*

Physiotherapist/Masseur: *Bob Stewart*

Physiotherapist/Masseur: *Stuart Barton*

Masseur: *Richard Wegrzyk*

Team Chef: *Dave Campbell*

Kit Technician: *Dave Tennisson*

Media Liaison: *Louisa Cheetham*

Specialist Advisor: *David McHugh*

Legal Officer: *Richard Smith*

— RUSSIA FINED —

Russia were fined £75,000 and expelled from the 2003 World Cup qualifying competition for fielding three ineligible Siberia-based South Africans – Renier Volschenk, Werner Pieterse and Johan Hendriks – in a qualifier against Spain. The fine was later rescinded, but the suspension stood.

— ERIC PETERS' HAT-TRICK —

There have been quicker hat-tricks of tries in England's Zurich Premiership – Dan Luger's seven-minute treble for Saracens against Rotherham in 2000 being one example – but Eric Peters' effort against Gloucester in February 1998 will take some beating for its unusualness. Peters, the Bath and Scotland back-row forward, came onto the field as a replacement for Dan Lyle after 70 minutes and scored in the 73rd, 76th and 81st minutes. He therefore scored a hat-trick inside nine minutes, having only been on the field for around 12!

— DOUBLE HONOUR —

Reginald Birkett, the scorer of England's first international try in 1871, was capped eight years later by England at soccer, too, and scored in a 5–4 victory over Scotland. Then, in 1880, he won an FA Cup winners' medal when his club, Clapton, beat Oxford University 1–0 in the final.

— FRENCH DOMINATION —

France enjoyed an early domination of Europe's second-tier competition, originally called the European Shield and now termed the European Challenge Cup. The first four finals were contested by French clubs, with Bourgoin beating Castres in 1997, Colombiers thrashing Agen in 1998, Montferrand overturning Bourgoin in 1999 and Pau making it second time unlucky for Castres in 2000. It took English club Harlequins to break the mould in 2001, when they beat Narbonne (yes, from France!) in a thrilling final that went into extra time.

— ANDY ROBINSON —

The man who succeeded Sir Clive Woodward as England head coach, Andy Robinson, has been given the toughest job in rugby: to win back-to-back World Cups. It has never been done before, but Robinson's career to date, as a teak-tough open-side flanker and hard-nosed successful coach, marks him out as someone it's difficult to bet against, as shown in his résumé below:

1987	Wins first of seven cup final victories with Bath.
1988	Makes England debut.
1989	Tours Australia with the British Lions.
1995	Wins eighth and final England cap.
1996	Gives up job as full-time teacher to become assistant coach at Bath.
1997	Promoted to chief coach by Bath.
1998	Guides Bath to thrilling Heineken Cup win.
2000	Takes over from John Mitchell as England coach.
2001	Tours Australia as assistant coach to Graham Henry on Lions tour.
2003	Wins Grand Slam and World Cup in role of England coach.

— TEN MORE FAMOUS RUGBY NICKNAMES —

Great White Shark – John Jeffrey
Bull of Dax – Laurent Rodriguez
Ginger Monster – Neil Jenkins
Lol – Lawrence Dallaglio
The Growler – Andy Robinson
Noddy – Michael Lynagh
Broon frae Troon – Gordon Brown
Merve the Swerve – Mervyn Davies
The King – Barry John
Shaggy – Will Greenwood

— JONNY'S GOALS —

What do you do when you're still only 24, have just won a World Cup winners' medal with a breathtaking drop goal, are the possessor of England's record number of points, have become a millionaire despite an aversion to publicity and are one of the few truly global superstars that rugby has produced? The answer, if you are Jonny Wilkinson, is that you simply set yourself new goals. Despite a 2004 that was bedevilled by injury, and which left many observers wondering if Wilkinson had a long-term future at all, here's what the man named as England's captain in succession to Lawrence Dallaglio still wants to achieve:

INTERNATIONAL RUGBY

- To win the World Cup again, and to be a major influence in the side that does it.

- To be selected for the British Lions tour to New Zealand in 2005, and to have an influence on a successful trip.

- To play as many games as possible, injury permitting.

- To win more Grand Slams.

- To be the best prepared player in the world.

- To play at his best in every match.

- To train at his best in every session, and never to accept that bad days just happen.

CLUB RUGBY

- To win the Zurich Premiership.

- To win it again.

- To win the Heineken Cup.

- To win the Powergen Cup.

- To dominate the game in England and Europe for several years.

- To lead Newcastle in that quest.

PERSONAL GOALS

- To become a better, more mature and developed person.

- To work with charities and make a difference to the causes that are close to him.

- To learn the guitar and piano.

- To become fluent in French and Spanish.
- To stay true to the ideal of being able to sign off the video of his life.

Wilkinson always pretends that his every waking minute is being videoed for posterity. It's his way of ensuring that he never cuts corners in training, for instance, or behaves badly.

— HIGHS AND LOWS 2 —

Heaviest and lightest players in the Zurich Premiership:

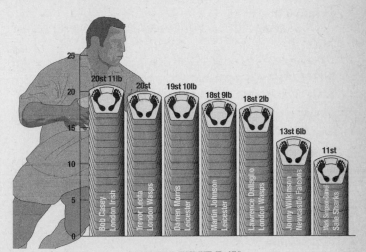

— CLIVE'S FIRST DAY —

What happened to Clive Woodward on his first day as England's inaugural professional head coach has already entered rugby legend. Turning up for work at the RFU headquarters at Twickenham, he was a little taken aback to find the staff there startled to see him. Then, to his disbelief, he found that there was neither an office nor a telephone available to him. Woodward's reaction? He began to work from the reception area, sharing cups of coffee (and a phone) with the receptionist. Unsurprisingly, an office was soon found for him.

— READY FOR BATTLE —

The moments before a big international are what most top-class players remember most vividly from their careers. Indeed, Martin Johnson said on his England retirement that he would cherish most the many memories of being in the dressing room both just before and just after the biggest games. In his recent book, *My World*, Jonny Wilkinson gives an insight into what happened in the England dressing room moments before the players emerged to beat Australia 20–17 and win the 2003 World Cup:

'It's just the players now. Johnno pulls us into a huddle. He talks passionately, telling us to look around at each other and remember the experiences we have been through together. This is our time. In the last year we have beaten everyone and overcome every challenge. It is this thought that we hold on to at this moment. Man for man, we believe we are better than Australia. We have worked harder than they have for this moment and we are stronger – physically and mentally. It is the game of our lives and there must be no regrets afterwards. No ounce of effort must be left behind.

'Lawrence Dallaglio and Phil Vickery chip in. Beneath the expletives, key points are being reinforced – it isn't just "let's kick the hell out of them". Nobody is punching or head-butting anyone. The fury is controlled. The aggression lurks just below the surface. It is there, though – I can feel it – and the adrenalin from that provides the last piece of comfort I need to go out there and attack the game. The thought of facing Australia in that furnace is frightening, but exhilarating too.

'Then it is time to go, time to face our destiny. We are held in a line, feet from the Wallabies, waiting for the signal to take the field together. In this situation, before every match I have ever played with him, Johnno has turned around and offered one final call to arms. He has the capacity to shock us and intimidate opponents with his venom and aggression, and I wonder what he is going to say. The Australia players will hear it as well and, with all the tension, it would not take much to light the blue touchpaper.

'Johnno turns around, fixes us with that beetle-browed stare and begins to open his mouth. But, for the first time, he does not say anything. That silence counts for a thousand words. He can see in our eyes that we are ready.'

— WAINWRIGHT'S MERCY DASH —

Former Scotland captain and back-row forward Rob Wainwright was also a qualified doctor, and during one match in 1995, when he was playing for West Hartlepool against Wasps at Sunbury, he rushed from the pitch to save the life of someone in the crowd. Wainwright helped to resuscitate a man who had just collapsed from a heart attack, and stayed with him until the paramedics arrived.

— JONES ON WOODWARD —

'It's a pity Clive isn't continuing in rugby. His role in raising the standards of preparation has been enormous and leaves a pretty big legacy to the game.'
> – *Australia coach Eddie Jones, a long-time verbal jouster with Woodward, reacting to the news that the 2005 Lions head coach plans to bow out of the game and turn to soccer following the tour.*

— BETSEN'S PHILOSOPHY —

All-action France flanker Serge Betsen, whose face bears the scars of an estimated 200-plus stitches, practises sophrology – a form of reflex mental conditioning under hypnosis – in an effort to stay more disciplined on the field. 'Putting together virtual game situations helps me to find the most suitable behaviour,' he says.

— TOP 20 BEST INTERNATIONAL POINTS PER GAME* —

		MATCHES	POINTS	SCORING AVERAGE
1	Jonny Wilkinson (England)	52	817 points	15.71
2	Grant Fox (New Zealand)	46	645	14.02
3	Andrew Mehrtens (New Zealand)	70	967	13.81
4	Daniel Carter (New Zealand)	17	232	13.65
5	Diego Dominguez (Italy)	74	983	13.28
6	Gonzalo Quesada (Argentina)	38	486	12.79
7	Michael Lynagh (Australia)	72	911	12.65
8	Jared Barker (Canada)	18	226	12.56
9	Paul Grayson (England)	32	400	12.50
10	Mike Hercus (USA)	23	286	12.43
11	Neil Jenkins (Wales)	87	1,049	12.06
12	Matt Alexander (USA)	24	286	11.92
13	Naas Botha (South Africa)	28	312	11.14
14	Gavin Hastings (Scotland)	61	667	10.93
15	Matthew Burke (Australia)	81	878	10.84
16	Nicky Little (Fiji)	53	574	10.83
17	Toru Kurihara (Japan)	35	377	10.77
18	Santiago Meson (Argentina)	34	364	10.71
19	Allan Hewson (New Zealand)	19	201	10.58
20	Braam van Straaten (South Africa)	21	221	10.52

* As at 1 January 2005

— THE LIONS JERSEY —

During the 1930 British Lions tour of New Zealand, there was an extraordinary sight to be seen. The New Zealand All Blacks turned out for the first Test at Dunedin in white jerseys, because those Lions were wearing blue shirts.

The colour clash that would have existed had the All Blacks worn their customary black shirts and black shorts, persuaded the touring Lions management that they should change permanently the colour of their shirts Thereafter, following that tour, the Lions always wore red jerseys (to denote Wales), with white shorts denoting England, and blue socks (for Scotland) with green tops to the socks (for Ireland).

— DORIAN WEST'S BENEFIT DINNER —

In early January 2004, Leicester and England hooker Dorian West held a benefit dinner with a difference. He persuaded half a dozen club colleagues to parade in drag outfits (evening wear and then swimsuit) in a spoof Miss Rugby World competition for an audience of 350 women. Unsurprisingly, it was a hilarious evening, much enjoyed by all, with one particular comment by a Leicester player (who must remain anonymous) bringing the house down. Dressed as 'Gloria Schwarzanegger from the Ukraine', this huge rugger-bugger was asked by the compère what 'she' thought about Ukrainian men. 'We don't touch them because, if we do, Chernobyl fall off' was the reported answer.

— ENGLAND EXPELLED —

The England team was actually expelled from the Five Nations Championship in 1999, although they were later reinstated in time to play in the tournament. The expulsion followed a dispute between the RFU and the other three home nations.

The dispute centred on the division of money that the RFU had received from a deal done in 1996 with a satellite television company. When the RFU agreed to sharing out certain monies, England were invited back into the tournament by the Five Nations Committee.

— KAY ON JOHNSON —

'Against Australia in Melbourne last summer we were driving a maul off a line-out and he stood on my face. I had to go off for stitches, and he laughed about it afterwards and said he did it on purpose. Then, in the French game at Twickenham, I was on the receiving end of his fist swinging into a maul. So, yeah, it's been great fun playing with him.'

– Ben Kay, fellow Leicester and England lock, paying tribute to Martin Johnson on the England captain's retirement from international rugby in January 2004.

— THE GOALPOSTS —

The height of the goalposts on a rugby pitch can be any height above the minimum of 3.4m (11ft). In practice, most are more than 7.5m but less than 9m in height (25–30ft). The distance between the two uprights must be 5.6m (18ft) and the bottom of the posts should be padded to make sure that the players don't injure themselves when colliding with them. The two posts should be joined by a crossbar 3m (10ft) above the ground – measured, that is, from the ground to the top edge of the crossbar. The crossbar must not extend beyond the posts.

— BIG BUSINESS —

The £3 million gross income generated by the first World Cup in 1987 produced a net profit of just £120,000. By 1991, that profit had grown massively to £25 million, from a gross income of £39 million. But income from sponsorship deals, which stood at around £10 million in 1991, had itself grown to almost £50 million by the 2003 tournament. The profit from the 1995 World Cup was £40 million, and this figure was doubled in 1999.

The 2003 World Cup, meanwhile, netted the International Rugby Board a whopping £150 million, while hosts Australia walked away with a net profit of around £20 million. In addition, the tournament added an estimated 300 million Australian dollars to the economy of New South Wales, where most of the 48 matches were staged. Big business, indeed.

— CRICKET'S INFLUENCE ON LIONS LEGACY —

Cricket had a significant role to play in the creation of an overseas British rugby touring team. The idea was dreamed up by two fine cricketers, Arthur Shrewsbury and Alfred Shaw, who had managed a cricket touring team to Australia in 1886/7.

Shrewsbury, the captain on that trip, was one of the most famous batsman of his day (legend has it that WG Grace used to say, 'Give me Arthur' – as his opening partner, that is – when later England selections were discussed), while Shaw was a former England captain who made many trips to Australia as both player and manager.

The two men were initially turned down when they suggested the idea of an overseas rugby team to tour in the southern hemisphere (or the southern colonies, as they were known in those days). The RFU refused to have anything to do with it, because it wasn't an officially designated touring team under their own auspices. In other words, because the RFU hadn't thought up the idea, they didn't want to know! But they didn't actively discourage the idea or the arrangements, which went ahead regardless.

However, because it wasn't an official, RFU-backed tour, many international players of the day didn't go. Shaw and Shrewsbury's solution was to choose players mainly from the north of England and the Scottish Borders, and this was duly done.

— BART'S BUM —

Thamesian RFC's veteran prop Bart Redmond was thrilled when a mate emailed him with the news that a picture of him was in the latest edition of *Rugby World* magazine. After rushing out to buy a copy, however, the well-built but hardly obese Redmond discovered that the main part of his anatomy featured in the photograph was his backside, in an advertisement for a product promising to 'significantly reduce body fat'.

— GREAT TRIES 4 —

ANDY HANCOCK
ENGLAND v SCOTLAND
TWICKENHAM, 1965

1   It's the final minute of this March encounter, and Scotland, leading 3–0, are heading for their first victory at Twickenham since 1938. David Whyte, the Scottish right wing, cuts inside and runs into a posse of English forwards about 15 yards in front of the home posts. A maul develops, and an unseen Englishman wrestles possession away from Whyte.

2   The ball is flung back to Mike Weston, the England fly-half. Sensing the need to attack even from this unpromising position, and that Whyte has been caught up in the maul, Weston instinctively switches to the blind side and throws out a long pass to left wing Andy Hancock.

3   Northampton's Hancock has been a peripheral figure for much of the match. Now, his isolation provides him with the chance of glory. Having dropped the only two passes he had been given previously, Hancock first concentrates on getting the ball safely into his hands before setting off up the wing. Several Scottish breakaway forwards come across the field at him, but he swerves back towards the touchline and sprints away.

4   The one Scotland player between him and the halfway line is the Scottish full back. Beating his tackle, Hancock is now in the clear, although various Scotland players are trying desperately to get to him.

5   On Hancock goes, over the heavy ground, and with main Scot Iain Laughland in pursuit. The crowd are willing him on, and he weaves inside and out in an effort to keep Laughland at bay. Just as he dives for the line, Laughland gets close enough to attempt the tackle. It has been a brave effort by them both, but Hancock's 95-yard solo run has taken him into the realms of rugby immortality, and England – despite a missed conversion from wide out – have saved the game 3–3.

Hancock, exhausted and later saying he can remember little about his length-of-the-field heroics, accepts a tot of whisky from an excited spectator as he drags himself off the field when the final whistle greets the missed conversion kick.

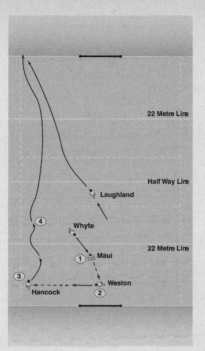

— JASON LEONARD IN A NUTSHELL —

114 England caps (1990–2004)

5 British Isles caps

4 Grand Slams

4 World Cup tournaments

3 British Isles tours

2 World Cup finals

2 matches as England captain

1 international try

1 World Cup winner's medal

— RECORDS OF BRITISH LIONS TEAMS —

RESULTS OF BRITISH AND IRISH LIONS

Opponents	Played	Won	Lost	Drew
South Africa	33	10	19	4
New Zealand	31	6	23	2
Australia	10	8	2	0

MOST POINTS BY THE LIONS IN A TEST SERIES

Points	Opponents	Matches	Year
79	South Africa	4	1974
68	South Africa	4	1980
59	South Africa	3	1997

MOST POINTS BY A LIONS PLAYER IN A TEST SERIES

Points	Player	Opponents	Matches	Year
41	NR Jenkins (Wales)	South Africa	3	1997
38	AG Hastings (Scotland)	New Zealand	3	1993
35	TJ Kiernan (Ireland)	South Africa	4	1968

MOST TRIES BY A LIONS PLAYER IN A TEST SERIES

Tries	Player	Opponents	Matches	Year
4	WM Llewellyn (Wales)	Australia	3	1904
4	JJ Williams (Wales)	South Africa	4	1974

MOST PENALTY GOALS BY A LIONS PLAYER IN A TEST SERIES

Penalties	Player	Opponents	Matches	Year
13	NR Jenkins (Wales)	South Africa	3	1997
12	AG Hastings (Scotland)	New Zealand	3	1993
11	TJ Kiernan (Ireland)	South Africa	4	1968

MOST DROPPED GOALS IN A TEST SERIES

Goals	Player	Opponents	Matches	Year
2	PF Bush (Wales)	Australia	3	1904
2	B John (Wales)	New Zealand	4	1971
2	P Bennett (Wales)	South Africa	4	1974

MOST CONVERSIONS IN A TEST SERIES

Conversions	Player	Opponents	Matches	Year
5	S Wilson (Scotland)	Australia	1	1966

MOST POINTS BY A LIONS PLAYER IN A TEST MATCH

Points	Player	Opponents	Venue	Year
18	AJP Ward (Ireland)	South Africa	Cape Town	1980
18	AG Hastings (Scotland)	New Zealand	Christchurch	1993
17	TJ Kiernan (Ireland)	South Africa	Pretoria	1968

MOST POINTS BY A LIONS PLAYER IN TESTS

Points	Player	Matches	Career
66	AG Hastings (Scotland)	6	1989–93
44	P Bennett (Wales)	3	1974–7
41	NR Jenkins (Wales)	3	1997

MOST TRIES BY A LIONS PLAYER IN A TEST CAREER

Tries	Player	Matches	Career
6	AJF O'Reilly (Ireland)	10	1955–9
5	JJ Williams (Wales)	7	1974–7
4	MJ Price (Wales)	5	1904

MOST POINTS SCORED BY THE LIONS IN A TEST MATCH

Points	Opponents	Venue	Year
31	Australia	Brisbane	1966
28	South Africa	Pretoria	1974
26	South Africa	Port Elizabeth	1974

LONGEST LIONS CAREER

Seasons	Player	Caps	Career
13	WJ McBride (Ireland)	17	1962–74

MOST CAPPED LIONS PLAYERS

Caps	Player	Career
17	WJ McBride (Ireland)	1962–74
13	REG Jeeps (England)	1955–62
12	CMH Gibson (Ireland)	1966–71
12	G Price (Wales)	1977–83

MOST POINTS SCORED BY THE LIONS VERSUS SOUTHERN HEMISPHERE TEAMS

Points	Opponents	Venue	Final Score	Year
28	South Africa	Pretoria	28–9	1974
20	New Zealand	Wellington	20–7	1993
31	Australia	Brisbane	31–0	1966

— RECORDS OF BRITISH LIONS TEAMS (CONT'D) —

MOST POINTS SCORED AGAINST THE LIONS BY SOUTHERN HEMISPHERE TEAMS

POINTS	OPPONENTS	VENUE	FINAL SCORE	YEAR
35	South Africa	Johannesburg	16–35	1997
38	New Zealand	Auckland	6–38	1983
30	Australia	Sydney	12–30	1989

— YOU CAN'T KEEP OLD ALBION DOWN —

Boredom on tour can always be a problem, even on a Lions tour. In New Zealand in 1966, the Lions got to the west coast of South Island and found themselves sitting around with very little to do late one Sunday afternoon. New Zealand's rugged west coast may be spectacular from a scenic point of view, but London's Bond Street or New York's Fifth Avenue it most certainly is not. The Lions party was split into two hotels, the Old Albion and the New Albion, both situated at either end of the one street running through the town.

One night, Irish duo Willie John McBride and Ronnie Lamont – both Northern Ireland men with a great sense of humour – sat down beside the fire at their hotel, the Old Albion, and one said mischievously to the other, 'Why do you think it is that we're put in the Old Albion, while that lot get the plush stuff at the New Albion?'

McBride and his fellow conspirator decided to do something about it. Wandering outside in the gathering gloom, they found a horse tethered on a small patch of grass close to the hotel, and a rusting old bicycle nearby. McBride mounted the bike, Lamont the horse, and the pair rode slowly down the main street to the side entrance of the New Albion. Once inside, they heard their team-mates' voices in the bar of the hotel.

Creeping upstairs as quietly as possible, the pair proceeded to ransack the room of every Lions player. Kit bags, clothing and personal effects were flung out of the bedroom windows, until it was all laying strewn across the garden. When McBride and Lamont had finished their ransacking, they crept back downstairs, remounted horse and bicycle and rode off back to the Old Albion.

The next morning, the story was splashed all over the pages of the local newspaper, and local radio stations were discussing the incident at great length. But the identity of the 'burglars' remained a secret until 2004 – 38 years later – when McBride wrote his life story and revealed the truth.

— LOMU-LESS ALL BLACKS TRAMPLE THE BOOKIES —

Spread-betting firm Sporting Index were left licking their wounds at the 1995 World Cup…after a match in which Jonah Lomu wasn't even playing. Lomu was the terrifying new star of the 1995 tournament, but the bookmakers paid the penalty for taking their collective eye off the ball when they heard that the New Zealand management had decided to rest him from their group match against minnows Japan. Badly underestimating what an All Blacks team – even without Lomu – would do to the plucky but under-powered Japanese, Sporting Index predicted that New Zealand would win by a margin of only 40–45. A large number of shrewd punters piled in on their victory being bigger than that, but even they couldn't believe their good fortune when the pumped-up All Blacks second-string team tore Japan apart to win 145–17. Those lucky punters picked up winnings that were a cool 83 times their original stake.

— DRAW FOR THE 2007 WORLD CUP —

England, the current holders of the trophy, are in the same group as South Africa for the 2007 World Cup tournament, hosted by France, and their clash is widely expected to provide the showpiece opening fixture of the tournament. Here's the full draw:

FIRST ROUND
Pool A: England, South Africa, Oceania 1, America 3, Repechage 2
Pool B: Australia, Wales, Oceania 2, America 2, Asia 1
Pool C: New Zealand, Scotland, Europe 1, Europe 2, Repechage 1
Pool D: France, Ireland, America 1, Europe 3, Africa 1

QUARTER-FINALS
Pool A winner v Pool B runner-up (1)
Pool A runner-up v Pool B winner (2)
Pool C winner v Pool D runner-up (3)
Pool C runner-up v Pool D winner (4)

SEMI-FINALS
(1) v (2)
(3) v (4)

FINAL
To be held on 20 October 2007 at the Stade de France, Paris

— ENGLAND'S FUEL —

A full-time chef has been part of England's support staff for some time now, thanks to the behind-the-scenes revolution of preparation laid down in the Woodward years. Here is a typical players' menu for a day spent at an England training camp:

BREAKFAST

Muesli, fruit, yoghurt

Egg-white omelette with smoken chicken and mushroom

— • —

LUNCH

Chunky vegetable soup

Choice of five salads

Grilled salmon with tomato sauce and couscous

Steamed vegetables

Fruit smoothie (eg mango and banana with protein mix)

— • —

DINNER

Chicken chowder with tiger prawns

Oriental salads

Pasta dish with mushroom and herb sauce and fresh vegetables
AND/OR
Low-fat mixed grill (lean steak, Bratwurst sausage, skinless chicken breast, tomatoes, sautéed mushrooms, Cajun potato wedges)

Wholemeal pancakes

Low-fat ice cream

— THE GREATEST MATCH EVER? —

Which match is the greatest in rugby's long history? Is it the 1999 World Cup semi-final between France and New Zealand? The 1973 Barbarians-versus-All Blacks thriller? The 1994 meeting of New Zealand and France in Auckland, which climaxed in the famous 'try from the end of the world'? Or what about one of the epic Lions tussles of the 1970s, or their 23–22 win against South Africa at Ellis Park during the 1955 tour? The candidates are many, and it's almost impossible to produce a definitive list because of all the imponderables of era, form, fitness, climate and occasion. Perhaps readers may wish to propose their own top ten, but here's a suggestion for the number-one match, purely in terms of entertainment value, skills levels and the massive size of the live audience that watched in awe when Australia played New Zealand in Sydney on 15 July 2000.

It was the deciding match of that year's Bledisloe Cup, and after just ten minutes of play the All Blacks led 24–0. Australia – the world champions from nine months earlier – reacted magnificently to this early blitz; their forwards decided to play keep-ball and, with the backs joining in, their players demonstrated the art of developing phase after phase of possession in breathtaking style. Suddenly, by half-time, the scoreline was locked at 24–24 and spectators knew that they had a classic on their hands.

New Zealand regained the lead early in the second half, but again the Wallabies responded, and a try from replacement hooker Jeremy Paul seemed to have clinched a 35–34 win. Only minutes remained and, amid huge tension and an atmosphere of enormous excitement being generated by a world record crowd of 109,874, the All Blacks raised themselves for one last effort. Flanker Taine Randell made a burst towards the touchline and drew two defenders to him. He then threw out a long basketball-style pass to Jonah Lomu, and the huge wing capped an epic contest by surging down the edge of the pitch in irrepressible fashion to plunge over in the corner.

'I doubt if there has been a better or more remarkable game of rugby ever played,' said Australia's captain and double World Cup winner John Eales afterwards, while one other player opined, 'It was fantasy-land stuff from start to finish,' after Lomu had delivered his dramatic *coup de grâce*.

— HUGO PORTA —

He won 49 caps for Argentina and eight more for the South American Jaguars in a Test career spanning an extraordinary 19 years. He scored 530 international points and is unquestionably the greatest rugby player to have emerged from South America.

Fly-half Hugo Porta was blisteringly quick over 10–15 metres and also a maestro when it came to distribution of the ball. His passing and kicking from hand were sublime, and in the 1980s he masterminded some of Argentina's greatest victories; the Pumas beat Australia in Brisbane in 1983 and then France in 1985, while in that same year the All Blacks were held 21–21. In addition, in 1982 Porta was a major influence in the Jaguars team that stunned the rugby world by beating South Africa 21–12 in Bloemfontein.

Porta was born on 11 September 1951, in Buenos Aires, and now works as the Argentine Ambassador to South Africa.

— GREAT TRIES 5 —

PHILIPPE SAINT-ANDRE
FRANCE v ENGLAND
TWICKENHAM, 1991

Philippe Saint-Andre's magnificent try was not enough to decide the Grand Slam showdown against England, but it still provided the most memorable passage of play in a game that France lost 21–19. Given the tension of the occasion, indeed, it stands for all time alongside Sadourny's 1994 try at Eden Park as a joint monument to French audacity and flair. It is fitting, too, that Saint-Andre – the finisher here, and the catalyst three years later – is able to provide the human link between the two great scores.

1   Serge Blanco, perhaps the greatest of all of France's electrifying backs, is
     the man who sets this classic counter-attacking try in motion. Weighing
     up the options in an instant, as he fields a loose kick ahead inside his own

in-goal area he dummies a touchdown and then sets off like a startled rabbit from behind the posts and away to his right.

2 Blanco sprints away and out of the French 22 before passing wide to Jean-Baptiste Lafond, the wing, who in turn finds Philippe Sella inside him.

3 Sella makes ground, and as he goes over the halfway line he passes outside him to the supporting Didier Cambarabero. The fly-half has done well to get there, but he doesn't have the pace to outflank England's desperate defence. Looking up, he cross-kicks perfectly…

4 …and Saint-Andre, who has sprinted the length of the field from his left-wing station, collects the bouncing ball safely before going over under the England posts.

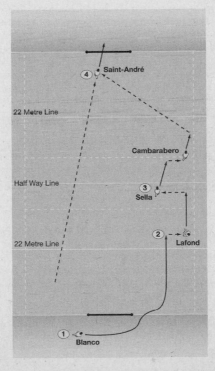

— CAMPO ON THE ALL BLACKS —

There has never been a more outspoken rugby voice than that belonging to the great former Australia wing David Campese. In his 1991 autobiography *On A Wing And A Prayer*, however, Campo gives an interesting insight into the magical quality of New Zealand Test rugby. He writes: 'When you play the All Blacks, you are playing the best in the world. They set themselves the very highest standards of performance as a norm, and if you cannot aspire to those peaks yourselves as a team, then you are gone. There is simply no place for the weak-hearted, for those short on confidence or self-belief. Theirs is a history of ruthlessly crushing any inferior opposition, and you know the stakes when you go out to face them.

'To win a Test match against New Zealand is to know a feeling of deep satisfaction and pleasure at the completion of a job well done. There is no other sense of elation comparable that I know of in all international sport. I can honestly say I've never seen a bad New Zealand side. There is an inherent ability in every New Zealand rugby team that goes out on the paddock, more so than in any other rugby-playing nation on Earth. Each and every team wearing the silver fern knows its task, it understands how much is expected of it, and it is formidably aware of the price of failure. That has been, and will always be, an enormous source of power and performance, for I don't believe there is a New Zealander born who does not understand all about the importance of the All Blacks doing well.

'People often ask me just what it is that marks out the All Blacks as so special on the rugby field. There is an intrigue, a mysticism about them on which they trade cleverly. They build this well of inner belief which touches every fibre of the player going out to represent New Zealand in a Test match. Filled with that sense of history, destiny and importance, is it any wonder that these guys play a rugby match as though their very lives depended on it?'

— FIVE/SIX NATIONS' YOUNGEST AND OLDEST —

The **youngest** player to have appeared in the championship is Ireland's Frank Hewitt, who made his debut in 1924, aged **17 years** and **157 days**.

The **oldest** player to have appeared in the Championship is Welshman Tommy Vile, who took to the field in 1921, aged **38 years** and **152 days**.

— THE BAJADA —

This is the name given to the eight-man scrummaging technique developed by the Argentina sides of the 1970s and 1980s. In world terms, only the French have ever possessed as many formidably strong scrummaging packs as the Pumas during the past four decades.

— LOMU'S ENTRANCE —

He had raised a few eyebrows in the Hong Kong Sevens, but the world at large saw Jonah Lomu for the first time only at the 1995 World Cup. He'd turned 20 just a fortnight before the tournament began, he was all but 18 stone, he stood 6 feet 5 inches tall…and he played on the wing. No New Zealand rugby pundit had included him in their likely World Cup squads, yet – like Campese at the 1991 tournament – he was to become the star of the show, taking the impact of wing play to yet another level.

In New Zealand's first match of the 1995 tournament, against Ireland in Johannesburg, Lomu scored two tries and made two more while winning just his third All Black cap. Setting up a try for flanker Josh Kronfeld, Lomu ran 80m and swatted four would-be tacklers out of his path as if they were irritant flies. It was to become the enduring image of the competition, with England's Tony Underwood and Mike Catt and Scotland's Gavin Hastings among those who felt the force of Lomu's juggernaut progress. One of the many wonders of South Africa's ultimate victory over New Zealand in the final itself was their ability to negate the Lomu factor.

— KICK BUT DON'T TOUCH! —

Early rugby football featured placers of the ball when a penalty or conversion kick at goal was attempted. In fact, the kicker wasn't allowed to touch the ball once it had been placed on the ground; that was the job of the placer. In modern rugby, a placer is used only when windy conditions make it easy for the ball to topple over. However, in American football, the Law that requires a kicker always to work in tandem with a placer has been retained.

— PREMIERSHIP FIRSTS —

- The first match in English rugby's Premiership was played at the Recreation Ground in Bath on 23 August 1997, with the home team being beaten 20–13 by Newcastle Falcons.

- Newcastle's Tim Stimpson scored the first points of the Premiership with a penalty, two minutes into that same match.

- The first try in the Premiership, however, was claimed by former England captain Will Carling in a match between Northampton and Harlequins at Franklin's Gardens which kicked off 15 minutes later that day. Carling scored for the 'Quins after four minutes of that game.

- Steve Lander refereed the first Premiership match, between Bath and Newcastle.

- London Wasps prop Will Green was the first player to chalk up 150 Premiership appearances for one club.

— IRB WORLD RANKINGS —

As on 1 December 2004, the top 50 rugby nations in the IRB World Ranking list looked like this:

1	New Zealand	90.90 points
2	Australia	88.58
3	England	86.59
4	South Africa	84.74
5	France	83.70
6	Ireland	82.61
7	Argentina	78.67
8	Wales	76.91
9	Scotland	74.65
10	Fiji	74.17
11	Italy	72.54
12	Samoa	70.13
13	Romania	68.61
14	Canada	68.12
15	Uruguay	66.92
16	United States	66.42

17 Portugal 65.77
18 Japan..65.00
19 Tonga 62.72
20 Georgia 61.08
21 Korea 60.25
22 Morocco 59.94
23 Namibia 59.38
24 Chile...58.79
25 Russia...58.19
26 Ukraine 57.66
27 Czech Republic 56.83
28 Hong Kong 55.50
29 Germany 55.16
30 Tunisia 54.09
31 Netherlands...53.49
32 Spain 53.43
33 Paraguay 53.18
34 Poland...52.70
35 Brazil..51.55
36 Chinese Taipei 50.93
37 Croatia..50.29
38 Moldova 49.21
39 Switzerland 49.08
40 Cote d'Ivoire 48.87
41 China 48.82
42 Denmark 48.31
43 Singapore 47.98
44 Madagascar..47.57
45 Sweden..47.42
46 Zimbabwe 47.36
47 Venezuela 47.33
48 Kazakhstan 46.86
49 Kenya 46.67
50 Belgium 46.55

— WHAT THE WORLD CUP WIN DID —

English rugby was celebrating the arrival of 33,098 new players one year on from the national team's historic Sydney victory against Australia in the 2003 World Cup final. A survey conducted by the Rugby Football Union in late 2004 indicated a 16 per cent growth in membership across all age groups, which took the numbers involved in club rugby to over 230,000. Based on a sample of 1,079 clubs, the RFU revealed that an additional 8,488 adults had taken up rugby following England's World Cup win, with 9,317 more participating at under-12 to under-18 level. However, the biggest increase was in the under-7 to under-11 age range, which saw growth to the tune of 15,293 players – a rise of 32 per cent. Around 500 clubs reported running at least one more team than a year earlier, and an additional 3,135 coaches and 783 referees were also recruited in the 12 months that followed Jonny Wilkinson's last-gasp dropped goal.

The RFU survey showed that, by the end of 2004, English rugby was being served by 22,469 coaches and 6,060 active referees, while the number of volunteers within the game had risen by 8.6 per cent, from 33,225 to 36,081. Such growth was even more welcome, however, because participation levels had actually fallen prior to the 2003 World Cup.

— WOODWARD ON WILKINSON —

'It was obvious he was a special talent from day one. He's just such a professional person and a great lad. It annoys me when everyone tries to break him down and psychoanalyse him. The guy is an outstanding talent who works incredibly hard. It's as simple as that.'
– *Sir Clive Woodward on Jonny Wilkinson*

— JARROD CUNNINGHAM —

In June 2002, London Irish player Jarrod Cunningham (then 33) was diagnosed with ALS, a form of motor neurone disease (MND) that brought a premature end to his fine rugby career. Jarrod had joined Irish in July 1998 after a successful career in his native New Zealand. Over three and a half seasons, he played 82 games for the Exiles, scoring 18 tries and 848 points. A creative and talented fly-half or full back, he was the leading points-scorer in the Zurich Premiership in the 1999–2000 season, with 324 points.

Early in 2003 Jarrod established the Jarrod Cunningham SALSA Foundation, founded to provide hope, inspiration and education about MND/ALS and support for fellow sufferers. Jarrod was presented with the IRB Spirit of Rugby Award at the International Rugby Board's awards ceremony in London in November 2004.

Cunningham said, 'I would like to thank London Irish, its staff and players, and its incredible supporters for their friendship and support over the past, difficult two years. I would also like to thank the wider rugby community for all that it has done to support me. I am enormously proud to have been part of a sport with such a generous and caring spirit.'

— DORIAN WEST'S SHIRT —

Philip Green, the billionaire owner of Arcadia and Bhs, paid £500,000 at a charity auction for a signed England World Cup 2003 shirt belonging to Leicester's Dorian West, the squad's third-choice hooker. Green had been attending a function at London's Natural History Museum organised by children's charity the Rainbow Trust a week after England's 20–17 win over Australia. Green, who discovered the identity of the shirt's owner only after the event, said, 'For me, who it is from was not relevant on the night. I was bidding for an England shirt from the final signed by all the players. It's something special. And they showed a film of these kids, and if you had some money you'd have given it, too.'

— THE BARON —

Italy prop forward Andrea Lo Cicero has the title of baron on his home island of Sicily, but he confesses, 'I rarely use it. I am a modern guy.' At 19 stones, he is one of the best loose-head props in the modern game, and is also an excellent kayaker and a national Greco-Roman wrestling champion.

— RUGBY TWINS —

Fraser Waters and Stuart Abbott both play in the centre for London Wasps (often as a partnership), both were born in South Africa but have played for England, and both attended the same prep school in Cape Town (although Waters was in the year above). They are also such good friends that they are nicknamed Tweedledum and Tweedledee at the club.

— THE BIG KICK-OFF —

If you were under the impression that the 2007 World Cup takes place in…well, in 2007, then you would not be exactly right. It has, in fact, already started.

The qualification process for the next global tournament actually began on 4 September 2004, in the unlikely setting of the Pyrenees. Andorra played Norway at the MICG ground in the centre of Andorra la Vella – the capital of the tiny principality – in the first of the 86 matches that make up the European qualifying competition alone. The match was handled by André Watson, a South African who is the only referee to have officiated at two World Cup finals.

— CLOCK-WATCHING —

At the beginning of rugby football history, there was no such thing as a time limit on the length of matches; indeed, at Rugby School, some games lasted up to five days, or even parts of those days. No mention of the length of rugby matches was made in the original Laws of the game, and it was left to the two captains to ask the referee to make a ruling on this aspect of the contest.

The first international match – between Scotland and England in Edinburgh in 1871 – was played 50 minutes each way. The first time two 40-minute halves were mentioned in the Laws was in 1926.

ENGLISH PREMIERSHIP CLUBS
— VITAL STATISTICS —

BATH RUGBY
Ground address: The Recreation Ground, Bath, BA2 6PW
Capacity: 9,980
Ticket info hotline: 0871 721 1865

Club honours: Heineken Cup 1997–8

> National League 1988–9, 1990–1, 1991–2, 1992–3, 1993–4, 1995–6

> National Cup 1983–4, 1984–5, 1985–6, 1986–7, 1988–9, 1989–90, 1991–2, 1993–4, 1994–5, 1995–6

GLOUCESTER
Ground address: Kingsholm, Kingsholm Road, Gloucester, GL1 3AX
Capacity: 13,000
Ticket info hotline: 0871 871 8781

Club honours: National Cup 1971–2, 1977–8, 1981–2, 2002–3

HARLEQUINS
Ground address: The Stoop Memorial Ground, Langhorn Drive, Twickenham, TW2 7SX
Capacity: 9,500
Ticket info hotline: 0871 871 8877
Club honours: European Challenge Cup 2000–1, 2003–4

> National Cup 1987–8, 1990–1

LEEDS TYKES
Ground address: Headingley Stadium, St Michaels Lane, Headingley, Leeds LS6 3BR
Capacity: 21,000
Ticket info hotline: 0113 278 6181

Club honours: None at senior level

LEICESTER TIGERS
Ground address: Welford Road, Aylestone Road, Leicester LE2 7TR
Capacity: 16,815
Ticket info hotline: 0870 128 3430

Club honours: Heineken Cup 2000–1, 2001–2

Zurich Premiership 1998–9, 1999–2000, 2000–1, 2001–2

National League 1987–8, 1994–5

National Cup 1978–9, 1979–80, 1980–1, 1992–3, 1996–7

LONDON IRISH
Ground address: Madejski Stadium, Reading, Berkshire RG2 0FL
Capacity: 24,200
Ticket info hotline: 0118 968 1000

Club honours: National Cup 2001–2

LONDON WASPS
Ground address: Causeway Stadium, Hillbottom Road, Sands, High Wycombe, Buckinghamshire HP12 4HJ
Capacity: 10,000
Ticket info hotline: 0870 414 1515

Club honours: Heineken Cup 2003–4

European Challenge Cup 2002–3

Zurich Premiership 2002–3, 2003–4

National League 1989–90, 1996–7

National Cup 1998–9, 1999–2000

NEWCASTLE FALCONS
Ground address: Kingston Park, Brunton Road, Kenton Bank Foot, Newcastle NE13 8AF
Capacity: 10,000
Ticket info hotline: 0871 226 6060

Club honours: Zurich Premiership 1997–8

National Cup 1975–6, 1976–7, 2000–1, 2003–4

NORTHAMPTON SAINTS
Ground address: Franklin's Gardens, Weeden Road, Northampton NN5 5BG
Capacity: 12,200
Ticket info hotline: 01604 581000

Club honours: Heineken Cup 1999–2000

SALE SHARKS
Ground address: Edgeley Park, Hardcastle Road, Edgeley, Stockport SK3 9DD
Capacity: 10,541
Ticket info hotline: 0871 222 0120

Club honours: European Challenge Cup 2001–2

SARACENS
Ground address: Vicarage Road, Watford, Hertfordshire WD1 8ER
Capacity: 22,000
Ticket info hotline: 01923 475222
Club honours: National Cup 1997–8

WORCESTER WARRIORS
Ground address: Sixways, Pershore Lane, Hindlip, Worcester WR3 8ZE
Capacity: 8,200
Ticket info hotline: 01905 459325

Club honours: None at senior level

— INDEX —